Traditional British Ballads

EDITED BY

Bartlett Jere Whiting

HARVARD UNIVERSITY

APPLETON-CENTURY-CROFTS, Inc.

New York

LIBRARY OF CONGRESS CARD NUMBER: 55-10557

PRINTED IN THE UNITED STATES OF AMERICA

CONTENTS

❀

OUTLAW BALLADS

SUPERNATURAL BALLADS

HUMOROUS BALLADS

INTRODUCTION

About forty years ago in a country town in Maine a group of boys, the writer among them, went to the woods in search of mayflowers. When the trailing arbutus proved to be more than usually elusive its absence was recompensed by an exchange of songs and stories, some of them of a nature not altogether suitable to the family circle. The youthful barnyard humor was in part familiar and is for the most part now forgotten, but one song clung and clings:

> As I came home the other night,
> As drunk as I could be,
> I found a horse within the stall
> Where my horse ought to be.
> "Oh wife, dear wife, why can't you be true to me?
> Whose horse is in the stall,
> Where my horse ought to be?"
> "You old fool, you damned fool,
> You son of a gun," said she.
> "That's nothing but a milking-cow my mother sent to me."
> I've travelled all around this world for twenty years,
> A hundred miles or more,
> But saddle on a milking-cow I never saw before.

There were more stanzas, increasingly forthright in expression and thanks in part to a repetitive pattern and thanks in part to impropriety I became then and there a link in the great chain of oral transmission, and also the collector of a popular ballad.[1]

---

[1] Without suggesting either comparison or contrast, it may be worth mentioning that a hundred years or so earlier John Greenleaf Whittier as a boy in Haverhill, Massachusetts, had heard at least the beginning of the same ballad from a tramp who was probably a Scot and certainly a horse thief. The ballad was later to become one of Whittier's characteristic and favorite forms but, perhaps fortunately, he did not use our ballad as a model for content.

Sometime later I heard my father sing, in his fashion, a song which began:

> "Where have you been a-walking,
>   Fair Andrew my son,
> Where have you been a-walking,
>   My own pretty one?"

> "Down by the green meadow,
>   Mother, make my bed soon,
> For I'm poison-ed to the *very* heart,
>   And I fain would lie down."

Although my father remembered only a portion of the song, one of his boyhood companions who had heard it from the same singer was able to furnish the whole. So it was that when I read the one-volume edition of Child's *English and Scottish Popular Ballads* not long before coming to college I found to my surprise and joy that I was the possessor of versions of "Lord Randal" (11) and "Our Goodman" (38), two rather dissimilar but plainly popular ballads. In college it was my fortune to have as my faculty adviser George Lyman Kittredge, who showed interest in "Fair Andrew" and ultimately put it in print. He was more reserved with regard to my "Our Goodman," which he said was not in its entirety of a nature to lend itself readily to publication.

Every generation of collectors has announced mournfully that ballad singing is a dying art and that the end of collecting is in sight. Ballad singing is far from dead today, and if the end of collecting is in sight it is because the texts collected will be increasingly suspect. Ballads originally found among the people and then perhaps improved are being put back in circulation by way of records and the radio. There is nothing new in this, however, since in the past printed ballads, whether from broadsides or songbooks, often found their way back into oral circulation.

Ballads brought from the mother country by the settlers have had a surprising vitality in America, especially in the more remote and isolated areas. Of the ballads in the present collection only seven—"Lord Ingram" (8), "Fair Janet" (14), "Glasgerion" (16), "Johnie Armstrong" (22), "Robin Hood and the Monk" (27), "Kemp Owyne" (33), "The Maid and the Palmer" (37)—have apparently not been found in North

America. Several of the others, however, are extremely rare or are preserved only in single, corrupt, or suspect versions. For the convenience of those interested in the number and geographical spread of the American versions, pertinent references are given to Coffin's invaluable monograph.

What is a ballad? Jesting Pilate after posing a more profound question would not stay for an answer, but we may not be so prudential. "A ballad is a song that tells a story." So far so good, but a ballad has more distinguishing characteristics. It is plain in diction and imagery, it tells an elemental story of universal appeal, it concentrates on a single incident, it is sparing of explanatory details and background, it often begins *in medias res,* it employs abrupt transitions, it makes free use of dialogue and calculated repetition, its emphasis is on action rather than reflection, it is associated with a tune which is often more stable than its text, and it tells its tale impersonally without author's asides or editorial comment. Generalizations, it has been wisely said, are rarely true, and definitions are often a Procrustean bed, so we must not be surprised or dismayed if any considerable selection of ballads shows exceptions even to such simple hallmarks as these. The makers of ballads did not have the benefit of a succinct compendium of rules. Nevertheless, the rules hold generally and that, if a definition or description is to be given at all, is as much as can reasonably be expected. Of course, it could be argued, has been indeed, that to attempt to define a ballad is otiose as well as embarrassing, and that the individual need only be advised to read ballads and judge for himself.

Any concept of a ballad, whether accepted as received or arrived at empirically, is to a considerable degree influenced by earlier collectors and editors. The group with which we are immediately concerned, the English and Scottish popular ballads, are often called Child ballads, from the great editor, Francis James Child, whose monumental collection did more than anything else to preserve the work of the past, to stimulate further work, and to permit critics to operate with some degree of safety with what had been hitherto a scattered and confusing body of material. We must not forget, however, that Mr. Child was inspired by Svend Grundtvig's edition of traditional Danish ballads, that Grundtvig had been influenced by William Motherwell, a Scottish collector who followed after Sir Walter Scott, who in his turn owed his enthusiasm for ballads to Bishop Thomas Percy's *Reliques of Ancient English Poetry*. There are many other names, some illustrious, some notorious, in the history of ballad scholarship, ranging from rigorous scholars to careless, even fraudulent, collectors, to all of whom the modern reader of ballads owes some degree of gratitude or charity. Good versions are best versions, but a bad version is better than no version. That it was Mr. Child who set the standard is established by the fact that few ballads have been suggested as additions to his canon (see Hodgart, pp. 19-25). When a new recruit is advanced, the recommendation is usually to the effect that this is as good as many ballads in Child. Despite the fact that only one of the nominations is really very good there is much validity in the criterion, for we must admit that there is dross in the Child collection. No one can assert the 305 ballads are of equal merit. Mr. Child himself was aware of the shoddiness of certain of his entries, as is implied in several of his headnotes and expressed plainly in some of his (mainly unprinted) letters. Certain versions of good ballads are inferior, and no reader should expect to go through the full or abridged Child with unabated zest. Nevertheless, as Dryden said of the *Canterbury Tales*, "Here is God's plenty."

How old are the ballads? If we were to determine our answer by the dates on which most of our texts were recorded we should reply, not old at all. Of the versions in Mr. Child's collection only a handful are demonstrably older than the seventeenth century and most belong to the eighteenth and nineteenth. The lateness of record has enabled some scholars to argue that the ballad is a relatively late development, and that those critics who held and hold that it flourished in the Middle Ages, say from 1000 on, are reasoning against the facts or rather against the absence of facts. The argument from silence is easy and it is also dangerous, especially when we are dealing with the Middle Ages. Most Anglo-Saxon poetry, including the finest, has come down to us in single copies, and yet few would assert that there were not once other copies of these and of more, perhaps many more, poems which have not survived. There are traces of many lost Old and Middle English literary works, and one need not hesitate to say that more still were lost without trace. Even without such a literary disaster as attended the dissolution of the monasteries, a manuscript was an ephemeral thing at best, and literary chitchat, while not absent, was not as widespread in the Middle Ages as we could wish. Chaucer was an esteemed poet in his own day and perhaps more so in the next century, and yet several of his works are lost, some of which we know by name and some of which, regretting their composition, he characterized as "many a song and many a leccherous lay," types not abounding in his surviving minor poems.

If the later history of ballads proves anything it proves that they were sung and that they were transmitted orally and reduced to writing or print only when there was a commercial or scholarly incentive. The same ballads have been written down from the song or recitation of illiterate or at least non-literary people in the eighteenth, nineteenth, and twentieth centuries, and though printed texts may have intervened in some cases, circumstances do not permit this to be a plausible general assumption. Despite Mrs. Hogg's direful statement to Scott, "They were made for singing an' no for reading; but ye hae broken the charm now an' they'll never be sung mair," ballads do not die out of oral circulation because they are written down, and neither is it safe to assume that because a ballad was first written down at a particular date it necessarily came into existence not long before that date. Perhaps it did, as some ballads are older than others, and sometimes the fact can be demonstrated by reference to or treatment of an historical event, though even here, as the headnotes to our selection of historical ballads show, the treatment of history in ballads is neither consistent nor often historical. If ballads exist orally after the initial recording they are precisely as likely to have existed prior to that event, and the exact length of time is indeterminable in either case for any given ballad. That we have many more Middle English non-narrative lyrics than ballads is certainly true, but secular lyrics were likely to be concerned with some aspect of courtly love and so appealed to a more literate group than did the ballads. Among the lyrics there is at least one from the thirteenth century, "De Clerico et Puella" (in Carleton Brown, *English Lyrics of the XIIIth Century*, Oxford, 1932, pp. 152-4), which has a strong story element. The poem is mainly dialogue in which a woman uses strong language and threats of paternal and fraternal vengeance to drive away an unwanted suitor. When he reminds her that they had kissed once in a window, she suddenly recognizes him as a former lover who had suffered sore wounds and forest exile for her sake. She immediately determines to be his love despite father, mother, and all her kin. Surely we have here a familiar ballad theme of lovers separated by family opposition and one which if continued could have a happy, unhappy, or mixed ending. Proverbially one swallow does not make a summer, but neither does it rule out the existence of other swallows.

What is the origin of ballads? By asking that question we confront ourselves with a problem fully as puzzling as "what song the Syrens sang or what name Achilles assumed when he hid himself among women," but perhaps like them "not beyond all conjecture." The battle over ballad origins has been often vehement, sometimes petulant, and occasionally dismal. At the calculated risk of oversimplification it can be said that the main issue has been as to whether ballads are popular or folk poems, or poems artistic or literary in origin and popular only through oral transmission. The very earliest scholars, often a courtesy title, to discuss ballads took them to have been composed and performed by minstrels when too weary or hurried to venture on a full-scale romance and, indeed, a few ballads do have obvious connections with medieval romance. Later a vague and confused theory arose to the effect that ballads were somehow spontaneously generated ("das Volk dichtet") by the folk, that is, by the entire populace of a community at a time when the intellectual and cultural levels were pretty much the same without regard for rank or fortune. Such men as Jacob Grimm and Herder receive credit for formulating this theory, but their formulation was never sufficiently formal as to be readily intelligible. Later still it was argued that ballads came into existence when a group of villagers in festive mood danced on the green or beach to the accompaniment of songs which they composed extemporaneously as they danced. That people did dance—indeed still do—to the music of their own singing is well attested, and it is also known that words were sometimes improvised to go with the tunes. To such a manner of composition have been ascribed certain ballad features: the refrain, which could be sung by the group as a whole after one, though not always the same, individual sang the stanza; the use of stock phrases and stock situations and the appearance in more than one ballad of the same stanza or stanzas; the use of incremental repetition, a device by which the action of a ballad is advanced by the recurrence of stanzas or groups of stanzas with only a minimum of changes. Incremental repetition, a phrase coined by F. B. Gummere, is admirably illustrated by "The Maid Freed from the Gallows" (5) and other ballads in this selection. This explanation of ballad origins has been called the communal theory (not perhaps a very happy designation) and among its chief exponents are Gummere and Kittredge in his succinct yet comprehensive preface to the shorter edition of the Child ballads. It must be emphasized that neither they nor their adherents ever maintained that any one of the extant ballads necessarily came into existence by the joint efforts of a dancing throng. They held only that ballads, of whatever merit, were once so composed and that the original process left its marks on the form and manner of the ballad. Opponents of the communal theory have rejected the idea of a dancing, singing, improvising throng and hold it to have as little relation to reality as does an opera bouffe. They maintain that ballads were composed as are other artistic poems, sonnets for example, and that they owe their peculiar characteristics to the fact that they were taken over by the common people and changed, not always for the better, during oral transmission by communal re-creation. Probably most of those who write about ballads today are opponents of the communal theory, and it must be admitted that a stout adherence to belief in the ordinary methods of poetic composition simplifies the discussion of ballad origins, if only to the extent that it eliminates a possibly perplexing mystery. Yet it is not safe to say that an apparently common-sense, even rational approach really answers all the questions. Ballads *are* different from other poems and communal re-creation does not wholly explain their individuality. Who, for example, were the original authors, those anonymous poets, not mute but certainly inglorious, who wrote their songs only to give them to the peasantry? Why, once in a way, especially since they are held to have done their work in fairly recent centuries, did they never venture into print under their own names? The noble poets of the Tudor period were held to consider publication beneath their dignity, but their authorship was known to their contemporaries. We may at least be thankful that no one so far has discovered that Lord Bacon or the Earl of Oxford wrote the ballads. Why have professional literary men, some of them well acquainted with popular ballads, been unable, with rare exceptions, to imitate them successfully? Have we not, perhaps, merely substituted one mystery for another? For the readers of this book the origin of ballads is relatively immaterial, since the main point is the existence of the ballads themselves and the emotional and aesthetic satisfaction which they bring. An unhappy by-product of the "reasonable" approach to ballad origins is a possibly unconscious tendency to deprecate them as literature.

Very few of the earlier collectors and students of ballads were interested in the tunes or competent to consider them, and as a consequence only in the present century has serious attention been given to ballad music. The former attitude was that though ballads were sung by the folk, they were to be read by the educated. Nowadays the knowledge that tune and text go together has led occasionally to the extreme position that ballad texts without music are like a horse without legs: interesting to look at from a distance but not capable of moving anyone. Although it is true that many of the American versions afford more delight to the ear than to the eye, this doctrine is very nearly as untenable as to maintain that because plays were written for the stage they offer little to the solitary reader. We do not need to go as far as Charles Lamb went when he argued, perhaps with his tongue a little way in his cheek, that to see a presentation of one of Shakespeare's plays was a hindrance rather than a help to appreciation, to insist that the test of time and the approval of critics is proof that ballads, even without music, are a part of English literature. This last must of course be regarded as very special pleading, since the nature of this series would not permit the luxury of musical notation and since the editor, to his occasional regret, can not distinguish one note from another either on paper or in the air. Professor Bertrand H. Bronson of the University of California is about to bring out a comprehensive and magisterial edition of the music of the Child ballads. For the person with a less specialized interest, there are many recordings of ballads available, but because of the ephemeral character of individual pressings no effort has been made to specify particular recordings, and the reader is urged to use the references given in the Bibliography or to consult the staff of any good music store.

The ballads in the present collection are taken from Mr. Child's collection and are printed with the kind permission of its publishers, Houghton Mifflin Company. The few alterations in which the editor has indulged are in typography and punctuation.

ROMANTIC BALLADS

❧

1

Captain Wedderburn's Courtship

Child 46 B; Coffin, pp. 59-60

The method by which the sudden Wedderburn wins the acquiescence of the lady (her name is Grizey Sinclair in version A) to his impetuous and frank wooing is reminiscent of the first three Child ballads, "Riddles Wisely Expounded," "The Elfin Knight," and "The False Knight upon the Road." Riddles, questions, and tasks are so common in folklore that it is inevitable that they should become a component part of some ballads. In several instances the interlocutor's life depends on satisfactory answers, but not in the present ballad where they are merely an intellectual means of turning a kidnapping into an elopement. Indeed, by the time we reach stanza 13 and observe the far from demonstrable statements which the lady accepts without demur, we are justified in thinking that she has already yielded in principle and is talking now only out of nervousness, habit, or perhaps a feeling that she ought to hold out for the stock.

"Captain Wedderburn's Courtship" has not been common in North America.

1 The Lord of Rosslyn's daughter gaed through the wud her lane,
    And there she met Captain Wedderburn, a servant to the king.
    He said unto his livery-man, "Were 't na agen the law,
    I wad tak her to my ain bed, and lay her at the wa."

1

2   "I'm walking here my lane," she says, "amang my fa-
       ther's trees;
    And ye may lat me walk my lane, kind sir, now gin ye
       please.
    The supper-bell it will be rung, and I'll be missd awa;
    Sae I'll na lie in your bed, at neither stock nor wa."

3   He said, "My pretty lady, I pray lend me your hand,
    And ye'll hae drums and trumpets always at your com-
       mand;
    And fifty men to guard you wi, that weel their swords
       can draw;
    Sae we'll baith lie in ae bed, and ye'll lie at the wa."

4   "Haud awa frae me, kind sir, I pray let go my hand;
    The supper-bell it will be rung, nae langer maun I stand.
    My father he'll na supper tak, gif I be missd awa;
    Sae I'll na lie in your bed, at neither stock nor wa."

5   "O my name is Captain Wedderburn, my name I'll neer
       deny,
    And I command ten thousand men, upo yon mountains
       high.
    Tho your father and his men were here, of them I'd stand
       na awe,
    But should tak ye to my ain bed, and lay ye neist the
       wa."

6   Then he lap aff his milk-white steed, and set the lady on,
    And a' the way he walkd on foot, he held her by the
       hand;
    He held her by the middle jimp, for fear that she should
       fa;
    Saying, "I'll tak ye to my ain bed, and lay thee at the
       wa."

7   He took her to his quartering-house, his landlady looked
       ben,
    Saying, "Monie a pretty ladie in Edinbruch I've seen;
    But sic 'na pretty ladie is not into it a':
    Gae, mak for her a fine down-bed, and lay her at the wa."

8 "O haud awa frae me, kind sir, I pray ye lat me be,
For I'll na lie in your bed till I get dishes three;
Dishes three mun be dressd for me, gif I should eat them
a',
Before I lie in your bed, at either stock or wa."

9 " 'Tis I maun hae to my supper a chicken without a
bane;
And I maun hae to my supper a cherry without a stane;
And I maun hae to my supper a bird without a gaw,
Before I lie in your bed, at either stock or wa."

10 "Whan the chicken's in the shell, I am sure it has na
bane;
And whan the cherry's in the bloom, I wat it has na
stane;
The dove she is a genty bird, she flees without a gaw;
Sae we'll baith lie in ae bed, and ye'll be at the wa."

11 "O haud awa frae me, kind sir, I pray ye give me owre,
For I'll na lie in your bed, till I get presents four;
Presents four ye maun gie me, and that is twa and twa,
Before I lie in your bed, at either stock or wa."

12 " 'Tis I maun hae some winter fruit that in December
grew;
And I maun hae a silk mantil that waft gaed never
through;
A sparrow's horn, a priest unborn, this nicht to join
us twa,
Before I lie in your bed, at either stock or wa."

13 "My father has some winter fruit that in December
grew;
My mither has a silk mantil the waft gaed never through;
A sparrow's horn ye soon may find, there's ane on
evry claw,
And twa upo the gab o it, and ye shall get them a."

14 "The priest he stands without the yett, just ready to
come in;

Nae man can say he eer was born, nae man without
  he sin;
He was haill cut frae his mither's side, and frae the
  same let fa;
Sae we'll baith lie in ae bed, and ye'se lie at the wa."

15 "O haud awa frae me, kind sir, I pray don't me per-
  plex,
For I'll na lie in your bed till ye answer questions six:
Questions six ye maun answer me, and that is four
  and twa,
Before I lie in your bed, at either stock or wa."

16 "O what is greener than the gress, what's higher than
  thae trees?
O what is worse than women's wish, what's deeper than
  the seas?
What bird craws first, what tree buds first, what first
  does on them fa?
Before I lie in your bed, at either stock or wa."

17 "Death is greener than the gress, heaven higher than
  thae trees;
The devil's waur than women's wish, hell's deeper than
  the seas;
The cock craws first, the cedar buds first, dew first on
  them does fa;
Sae we'll baith lie in ae bed, and ye'se lie at the wa."

18 Little did this lady think, that morning whan she raise,
That this was for to be the last o a' her maiden days.
But there's na into the king's realm to be found a
  blither twa,
And now she's Mrs. Wedderburn, and she lies at the
  wa.

[The last line of (A) reads: And she maun lye in his bed,
  but she'll not lye neist the wa]

2

Young Beichan

Child 53 A; Coffin pp. 63-5

Like the two which follow it, this ballad is graced by a
hero somewhat less than ideal as a lover and by a heroine
endowed with patience and persistence beyond the ordinary.
A few of the versions, of which there are many from Britain
and America, explain that Young Beichan was coerced into
marriage, but in most he seems to have entered upon matrimony without a thought of his earlier vow. A delightful instance of Mr. Child's tenderness for the characters in his
favorite ballads is to be found in his comment on Young
Beichan's inconstancy, which he thought or hoped might have
been due in the earliest form to magic: "for myself, I have
little doubt that, if we could go back far enough, we should
find that he had all along been faithful at heart" (I, 461). A
less kind explanation would be that after the outrageous
boast of stanza 6 he was a little ashamed to have the lady
perceive the truth. Some of the lives of Thomas Becket tell
a similar story about the saint's father. The legend and
the ballad are very like, but though the heathen lady pro-
poses to Gilbert Becket he escapes without her aid, and
indeed, his urge to escape is quickened by distrust of the
lady's advances. Then, too, Becket is neither engaged in or
contemplating matrimony when the lady arrives in London
and only marries her on the advice of a number of bishops
who correctly scent a miraculous occurrence and blessed
birth.

1   In London city was Bicham born,
        He longd strange countries for to see,
    But he was taen by a savage Moor,
        Who handld him right cruely.

2   For thro his shoulder he put a bore,
     An thro the bore has pitten a tree,
   An he's gard him draw the carts o wine,
     Where horse and oxen had wont to be.

3   He's casten [him] in a dungeon deep,
     Where he coud neither hear nor see;
   He's shut him up in a prison strong,
     An he's handld him right cruely.

4   O this Moor he had but ae daughter,
     I wot her name was Shusy Pye;
   She's doen her to the prison-house,
     And she's calld Young Bicham one word by.

5   "O hae ye ony lands or rents,
     Or citys in your ain country,
   Coud free you out of prison strong,
     An coud maintain a lady free?"

6   "O London city is my own,
     An other citys twa or three,
   Coud loose me out o prison strong
     An coud maintain a lady free.

7   O she has bribed her father's men
     Wi meikle goud and white money,
   She's gotten the key o the prison doors,
     An she has set Young Bicham free.

8   She's gi'n him a loaf o good white bread,
     But an a flask o Spanish wine,
   An she bad him mind on the ladie's love
     That sae kindly freed him out o pine.

9   "Go set your foot on good ship-board,
     An haste you back to your ain country,
   An before that seven years has an end,
     Come back again, love, and marry me."

10   It was long or seven years had an end
     She longd fu sair her love to see;

She's set her foot on good ship-board,
    An turnd her back on her ain country.

11   She's saild up, so has she doun,
    Till she came to the other side;
She's landed at Young Bicham's gates,
    An I hop this day she sal be his bride.

12   "Is this Young Bicham's gates?" says she,
    "Or is that noble prince within?"
"He's up the stairs wi his bonny bride,
    An monny a lord and lady wi him."

13   "O has he taen a bonny bride,
    An has he clean forgotten me!"
An sighing said that gay lady,
    I wish I were in my ain country!

14   But she's pitten her han in her pocket,
    An gin the porter guineas three;
Says, "Take ye that, ye proud porter,
    An bid the bridegroom speak to me."

15   O whan the porter came up the stair,
    He's fa'n low down upon his knee:
"Won up, won up, ye proud porter,
    An what makes a' this courtesy?"

16   "O I've been porter at your gates
    This mair nor seven years an three,
But there is a lady at them now
    The like of whom I never did see.

17   "For on every finger she has a ring,
    An on the mid-finger she has three,
An there's as meikle goud aboon her brow
    As woud buy an earldome o lan to me."

18   Then up it started Young Bicham,
    An sware so loud by Our Lady,
"It can be nane but Shusy Pye,
    That has come oer the sea to me."

19 O quickly ran he down the stair,
        O fifteen steps he has made but three;
    He's tane his bonny love in his arms,
        An a wot he kissed her tenderly.

20 "O hae you tane a bonny bride?
        An hae you quite forsaken me?
    An hae ye quite forgotten her
        That gae you life an liberty?"

21 She's lookit oer her left shoulder
        To hide the tears stood in her ee;
    "Now fare thee well, Young Bicham," she says
        "I'll strive to think nae nair on thee."

22 "Take back your daughter, madam," he says,
        "An a double dowry I'll gi her wi;
    For I maun marry my first true love,
        That's done and suffered so much for me."

23 He's take his bonny love by the han,
        And led her to yon fountain stane;
    He's changd her name frae Shusy Pye,
        And he's cald her his bonny love, Lady Jane.

3

Fair Annie

Child 62 A; Coffin, p. 69

That "Fair Annie" has seldom been recorded in the United
States may perhaps be ascribed to natural chivalry and an
aversion to illicit unions. The story was, however, widespread
in the Old World, one of the earliest treatments being in
Marie de France's *Lai le Fraisne* (before 1187), which appeared in an English translation early in the fourteenth century. In the lay the heroine is a twin, exposed at birth because

her mother fears that her own reputation may be injured by a double birth. She is found near a nunnery and brought up by its abbess, from whose care she is lured by the hero whose particular form of shabbiness is to discard her in due time because she is childless, a charge which could hardly have been brought against Fair Annie. He then, of course, marries the other twin, but the *contretemps* or coincidence is discovered in time to have the marriage annulled before consummation. Some critics of "Fair Annie" have been puzzled by the hero's temerity in seeking marriage with the sister of his mistress, but the reason lies in the earlier stages of the story when he was unaware of the relationship as, until the end, were the two sisters. The ballad hero, one uses the term conventionally, with his craving for gold and gear, is more reprehensible than his prototype in the lay.

1 "It's narrow, narrow make your bed,
    And learn to lie your lane;
For I'm ga'n oer the sea, Fair Annie,
    A braw bride to bring hame.
Wi her I will get gowd and gear;
    Wi you I neer got nane.

2 "But wha will bake my bridal bread,
    Or brew my bridal ale?
And wha will welcome my brisk bride,
    That I bring oer the dale?"

3 "It's I will bake your bridal bread,
    And brew your bridal ale,
And I will welcome your brisk bride,
    That you bring oer the dale."

4 "But she that welcomes my brisk bride
    Maun gang like maiden fair;
She maun lace on her robe sae jimp,
    And braid her yellow hair."

5 "But how can I gang maiden-like,
    When maiden I am nane?
Have I not born seven sons to thee,
    And am with child again?"

6   She's taen her young son in her arms,
     Another in her hand,
And she's up to the highest tower,
     To see him come to land.

7   "Come up, come up, my eldest son,
     And look oer yon sea-strand,
And see your father's new-come bride,
     Before she come to land."

8   "Come down, come down, my mother dear,
     Come frae the castle wa!
I fear, if langer ye stand there,
     Ye'll let yoursell down fa."

9   And she gaed down, and farther down,
     Her love's ship for to see,
And the topmast and the mainmast
     Shone like the silver free.

10   And she's gane down, and farther down,
     The bride's ship to behold,
And the topmast and the mainmast
     They shone just like the gold.

11   She's taen her seven sons in her hand,
     I wot she didna fail;
She met Lord Thomas and his bride,
     As they came oer the dale.

12   "You're welcome to your house, Lord Thomas,
     You're welcome to your land;
You're welcome with your fair ladye,
     That you lead by the hand.

13   "You're welcome to your ha's, ladye,
     You're welcome to your bowers;
You're welcome to your hame, ladye,
     For a' that's here is yours."

14   "I thank thee, Annie; I thank thee, Annie,
     Sae dearly as I thank thee;

You're the likest to my sister Annie,
That ever I did see.

15 "There came a knight out oer the sea,
And steald my sister away;
The shame scoup in his company,
And land whereer he gae!"

16 She hang ae napkin at the door,
Another in the ha,
And a' to wipe the trickling tears,
Sae fast as they did fa.

17 And aye she served the lang tables,
With white bread and with wine,
And aye she drank the wan water,
To had her colour fine.

18 And aye she served the lang tables,
With white bread and with brown;
And ay she turned her round about,
Sae fast the tears fell down.

19 And he's taen down the silk napkin,
Hung on a silver pin,
And aye he wipes the tear trickling
A' down her cheik and chin.

20 And aye he turn'd him round about,
And smil'd amang his men;
Says, "Like ye best the old ladye,
Or her that's new come hame?"

21 When bells were rung, and mass was sung,
And a' men bound to bed,
Lord Thomas and his new-come bride
To their chamber they were gaed.

22 Annie made her bed a little forbye,
To hear what they might say;
"And ever alas!" Fair Annie cried,
"That I should see this day!

23   "Gin my seven sons were seven young rats,
         Running on the castle wa,
      And I were a grey cat mysell,
         I soon would worry them a'.

24   "Gin my seven sons were seven young hares,
         Running oer yon lilly lee,
      And I were a grew hound mysell,
         Soon worried they a' should be."

25   And wae and sad Fair Annie sat
         And drearie was her sang,
      And ever, as she sobbd and grat,
         "Wae to the man that did the wrang!"

26   "My gown is on," said the new-come bride,
         "My shoes are on my feet,
      And I will to Fair Annie's chamber,
         And see what gars her greet.

27   "What ails ye, what ails ye, Fair Annie,
         That ye make sic a moan?
      Has your wine barrels cast the girds,
         Or is your white bread gone?

28   "O wha was't was your father, Annie,
         Or wha was't was your mother?
      And had ye ony sister, Annie,
         Or had ye ony brother?"

29   "The Earl of Wemyss was my father,
         The Countess of Wemyss my mother;
      And a' the folk about the house
         To me were sister and brother."

30   "If the Earl of Wemyss was your father,
         I wot sae was he mine;
      And it shall not be for lack o gowd
         That ye your love sall tine.

31   "For I have seven ships o mine ain,
         A' loaded to the brim,

And I will gie them a' to thee,
    Wi four to thine eldest son:
But thanks to a' the powers in heaven
    That I gae maiden hame!"

4

Child Waters

Child 63 A; Coffin, p. 70

This ballad has survived in America only in a version from North Carolina and a fragment from Missouri. Mr. Child called it "this charming ballad, which has perhaps no superior in English, and if not in English perhaps nowhere," but with characteristic prudence he added a footnote: "Caution is imperative where so much ground is covered, and no man should be confident that he can do absolute justice to poetry in a tongue that he was not born to; but foreign poetry is as likely to be rated too high as to be undervalued." He wanted to think, however, that the episode in stanzas 28-30, which is found in A alone "may be an insertion of some unlucky singer." Even without this deplorable incident Child Waters is a rather nasty fellow, and the fact that he was a woe man to see Fair Ellen swim implies not so much compassion as a strong desire to rid himself, no matter by field or flood, of a paramour who had become an embarrassment. If his mother had not been in the castle one suspects that Ellen would have spent more time in the stable than she did.

1   Childe Watters in his stable stoode,
        And stroaket his milke-white steede;
    To him came a faire young ladye
        As ere did weare womans weede.

2   Saies, "Christ you save, good Chyld Waters!"
    Sayes, "Christ you save and see!

My girdle of gold, which was too longe,
 Is now to short for mee.

3 "And all is with one chyld of yours,
  I feele sturre att my side;
 My gowne of greene, it is to strayght;
  Before it was to wide."

4 "If the child be mine, Faire Ellen," he sayd, — *commonplace – rythyme*
  "Be mine, as you tell mee,
 Take you Cheshire and Lancashire both,
  Take them your owne to bee.

5 "If the child be mine, Faire Ellen," he sayd, *simple &*
  "Be mine, as you doe sweare, ——— *incommental*
 Take you Cheshire and Lancashire both, *rhyme*
  And make that child your heyre." *repitition*

6 Shee saies, "I had rather have one kisse,
  Child Waters, of thy mouth,
 Then I wold have Cheshire and Lancashire both,
  That lyes by north and south.

7 "And I had rather have a twinkling,
  Child Waters, of your eye,
 Then I wold have Cheshire and Lancashire both,
  To take them mine oune to bee."

8 "To-morrow, Ellen, I must forth ryde
  Soe farr into the north countrye;
 The fairest lady that I can find,
  Ellen, must goe with mee."
 "And ever I pray you, Child Watters,
  Your footpage let me bee!"

9 "If you will my footpage be, Ellen,
  As you doe tell itt mee,
 Then you must cutt your gownne of greene
  An inche above your knee.

10 "Soe must you doe your yellow lockes,
  Another inch above your eye;

You must tell noe man what is my name;
My footpage then you shall bee."

11   All this long day Child Waters rode,
        Shee ran bare foote by his side;
     Yett was he never soe curteous a knight
        To say, "Ellen, will you ryde?"

12   But all this day Child Waters rode,
        Shee ran barfoote thorow the broome;
     Yett he was never soe curteous a knight
        As to say, "Put on your shoone."

13   "Ride softlye," shee said, "Child Waters;
        Why doe you ryde soe fast?
     The child which is no mans but yours
        My bodye itt will burst."

14   He sayes, "Sees thou yonder water, Ellen,
        That flowes from banke to brim?"
     "I trust to God, Child Waters," shee said,
        You will never see mee swime."

15   But when shee came to the waters side,
        Shee sayled to the chinne:
     "Except the lord of heaven be my speed,
        Now must I learne to swime."

16   The salt waters bare up Ellens clothes,
        Our Ladye bare upp her chinne,
     And Child Waters was a woe man, good Lord,
        To see Faire Ellen swime.

17   And when shee over the water was,
        Shee then came to his knee:
     He said, "Come hither, Faire Ellen,
        Loe yonder what I see!

18   "Seest thou not yonder hall, Ellen?
        Of redd gold shine the yates;
     There's four and twenty fayre ladyes,
        The fairest is my wordlye make.

19   "Seest thou not yonder hall, Ellen?
        Of redd gold shineth the tower;
     There is four and twenty faire ladyes,
        The fairest is my paramoure."

20   "I doe see the hall now, Child Waters,
        That of redd gold shineth the yates;
     God give good then of your selfe,
        And of your wordlye make!

21   "I doe see the hall now, Child Waters,
        That of redd gold shineth the tower;
     God give good then of your selfe,
        And of your paramoure!"

22   There were four and twenty ladyes,
        Were playing att the ball,
     And Ellen, was the fairest ladye,
        Must bring his steed to the stall.

23   There were four and twenty faire ladyes
        Was playing att the chesse;
     And Ellen, shee was the fairest ladye,
        Must bring his horsse to grasse.

24   And then bespake Child Waters sister,
        And these were the words said shee:
     "You have the prettyest footpage, brother,
        That ever I saw with mine eye;

25   "But that his belly it is soe bigg,
        His girdle goes wonderous hye;
     And ever I pray you, Child Waters,
        Let him goe into the chamber with mee."

26   "It is more meete for a little footpage,
        That has run through mosse and mire,
     To take his supper upon his knee
        And sitt downe by the kitchin fyer,
     Then to goe into the chamber with any ladye
        That weares soe [rich] attyre."

27 But when thé had supped every one,
 To bedd they took the way;
 He sayd, "Come hither, my little footpage,
  Harken what I doe say.

28 "And goe thee downe into yonder towne,
 And low into the street;
 The fairest ladye that thou can find,
  Hyer her in mine armes to sleepe,
 And take her up in thine armes two,
  For filinge of her feete.

29 Ellen is gone into the towne,
 And low into the streete;
 The fairest ladye that shee cold find
  Shee hyred in his armes to sleepe,
 And tooke her in her armes two,
  For filinge of her feete.

30 "I pray you now, good Child Waters,
 That I may creepe in att your bedds feete;
 For there is noe place about this house
  Where I may say a sleepe."

31 This [night] and itt drove on affterward
 Till itt was neere the day:
 He sayd, "Rise up, my little ffoote-page,
  And give my steed corne and hay;
 And soe doe thou the good blacke oates,
  That he may carry me the better away."

32 And up then rose Faire Ellen,
 And gave his steed corne and hay,
 And soe shee did and the good blacke oates,
  That he might carry him the better away.

33 Shee layned her backe to the manger side,
 And greivouslye did groane;
 And that beheard his mother deere,
  And heard her make her moane.

triumph of incremental repetition over sense and taste, and for that reason it is found in this selection. Continental versions are better in that some background is given: the girl has been captured by pirates and her family refuse to pay the ransom demanded. In the North American versions the hangman is substituted for the judge, and in a few cases we are told that the heroine has stolen or lost some precious object. When one observes the unanimity with which her immediate family flock to see her hanged one thinks that perhaps the true-love should be a little cautious before he commits himself too permanently unless, of course, we are confronted with an Edwards unexpectedly born into the Jukes family.

1   "O good Lord Judge, and sweet Lord Judge,
      Peace for a little while!
    Methinks I see my own father,
      Come riding by the stile.

2   "Oh father, oh father, a little of your gold,
      And likewise of your fee!
    To keep my body from yonder grave,
      And my neck from the gallows-tree."

3   "None of my gold now you shall have,
      Nor likewise of my fee;
    For I am come to see you hangd,
      And hanged you shall be."

4   "Oh good Lord Judge, and sweet Lord Judge,
      Peace for a little while!
    Methinks I see my own mother,
      Come riding by the stile.

5   "Oh mother, oh mother, a little of your gold,
      And likewise of your fee,
    To keep my body from yonder grave,
      And my neck from the gallows-tree!"

6   "None of my gold now shall you have,
      Nor likewise of my fee,

For I am come to see you hangd,
And hanged you shall be."

7 Oh good Lord Judge, and sweet Lord Judge,
Peace for a little while!
Methinks I see my own brother,
Come riding by the stile.

8 "Oh brother, oh brother, a little of your gold,
And likewise of your fee,
To keep my body from yonder grave,
And my neck from the gallows-tree!"

9 "None of my gold now shall you have,
Nor likewise of my fee;
For I am come to see you hangd,
And hanged you shall be."

10 "Oh good Lord Judge, and sweet Lord Judge,
Peace for a little while!
Methinks I see my own sister,
Come riding by the stile.

11 "Oh sister, oh sister, a little of your gold,
And likewise of your fee,
To keep my body from yonder grave,
And my neck from the gallows-tree!"

12 "None of my gold now shall you have,
Nor likewise of my fee;
For I am come to see you hangd,
And hanged you shall be."

13 "Oh good Lord Judge, and sweet Lord Judge,
Peace for a little while!
Methinks I see my own true-love,
Come riding by the stile.

14 "Oh true-love, oh true-love, a little of your gold,
And likewise of your fee,
To save my body from yonder grave,
And my neck from the gallows-tree."

15 "Some of my gold now you shall have,
       And likewise of my fee,
   For I am come to see you saved,
       And saved you shall be."

6

The Gipsy Laddie

Child 200 B; Coffin, pp. 120-4

This ballad could fall into more than one of our categories.
The glamourie which the gypsies cast over the lady gives
it a supernatural tinge, perhaps more evident in the original
form. Jackie or Johnnie Faa was among the gypsies a common name, often held by men fated to execution, and earlier
commentators considered, without too much reason, that the
ballad was historical. Our version, along with a majority of
the British, ends with the death of the gypsies, which is
tragedy indeed for them and presumably for the lady. It is
placed among the romances here out of deference to the
fact that in most of the North American versions the husband is rebuffed, and the lady goes on in love if not comfort
with her black Jack gypsy O. Any conventional sympathy
that we may feel for the husband is dispelled in several
versions when he makes her return various articles of orna-
ment or attire, including all too often her shoes.

1 The gypsies they came to my lord Cassilis' yett,
       And O but they sang bonnie!
   They sang so sweet and so complete
       Till down came our fair ladie.

2 She came tripping down the stairs,
       And all her maids before her;
   As soon as they saw her weel-far'd face,
       They cast their glamourie owre her.

3 She gave them the good wheat bread,
    And they gave her the ginger;
But she gave them a fair better thing,
    The gold rings of her fingers.

4 "Will ye go with me, my hinny and my heart?
    Will you go with me, my dearie?
And I will swear by the hilt of my spear,
    That your lord shall no more come near thee."

5 "Gar take from me my silk manteel,
    And bring to me a plaidie,
For I will travel the world owre
    Along with the gypsie laddie.

6 "I could sail the seas with my Jackie Faa,
    I could sail the seas with my dearie;
I could sail the seas with my Jackie Faa,
    And with pleasure could drown with my dearie."

7 They wandred high, they wandred low,
    They wandred late and early,
Untill they came to an old farmer's barn,
    And by this time she was weary.

8 "Last night I lay in a weel-made bed,
    And my noble lord beside me,
And now I most ly in an old farmer's barn,
    And the black crae glowring owre me."

9 "Hold your tongue, my hinny and my heart,
    Hold your tongue, my dearie,
For I will swear, by the moon and the stars,
    That thy lord shall no more come near thee."

10 They wandred high, they wandred low,
    They wandred late and early,
Untill they came to that on water,
    And by this time she was wearie.

11 "Many a time I have rode that on water,
    And my lord Cassilis beside me,

And now I must set in my white feet and wade,
   And carry the gypsie laddie."

12 By and by came home this noble lord,
       And asking for his ladie,
    The one did cry, the other did reply,
       "She is gone with the gypsie laddie."

13 "Go saddle to me the black," he says,
       "The brown rides never so speedie,
    And I will neither eat nor drink
       Till I bring home my ladie."

14 He wandred high, he wandred low,
       He wandred late and early,
    Untill he came to that on water,
       And there he spied his ladie.

15 "O wilt thou go home, my hinny and my heart,
       O wilt thou go home, my dearie?
    And I'll close thee in a close room,
       Where no man shall come near thee."

16 "I will not go home, my hinny and my heart,
       I will not go home, my dearie;
    If I have brewn good beer, I will drink of the same,
       And my lord shall no more come near me.

17 "But I will swear, by the moon and the stars,
       And the sun that shines so clearly,
    That I am as free of the gypsie gang
       As the hour my mother bore me."

18 They were fifteen valiant men,
       Black, but very bonny,
    They lost all their lives for one,
       The Earl of Cassillis' ladie.

TRAGIC BALLADS

❧

7

Edward

Child 13 A and B; Coffin, pp. 45-6

At least since Motherwell scholars have voiced the suspicion that David Dalrymple, Lord Hailes, who gave the B copy to Percy, improved the text which he transmitted. Certainly the spellings are "affectedly antique," though more so in Percy than in Child, and certainly the climax differs from the other versions. Perhaps Lord Hailes did take liberties with the poem, but so far as the spellings are concerned it is curious to observe that a few years later (1780) when he edited a selection of poems from the Bannatyne Manuscript he made an editorial stricture on the "general error" of using 3 instead of the y of the Anglo-Saxons, a feature of Percy's print which Child removed. Whatever their feeling about its composition all critics agree that the B text is one of the finest of ballads. The tragic surprise of the last stanza imparts its shock even after many readings or hearings. Probably it should be noted that in later versions the mother is relieved of any complicity in the crime, which thus becomes no more than a murderous quarrel over a trivial cause. "Edward" has been not infrequent in North America. For special studies see Archer Taylor, *"Edward" and "Sven i Rosengård," A Study in the Dissemination of a Ballad,* Chicago, 1931; Bertrand H. Bronson, "Edward Edward, A Scottish Ballad," *Southern Folklore Quarterly* IV (1940), 1-13, 159-61.

(A)

1 "What bluid's that on thy coat lap,
   Son Davie, son Davie?

What bluid's that on thy coat lap?
 And the truth come tell to me."

2 "It is the bluid of my great hawk,
  Mother lady, mother lady:
 It is the bluid of my great hawk,
  And the truth I have told to thee."

3 "Hawk's bluid was neer sae red,
  Son Davie, son Davie:
 Hawk's bluid was neer sae red,
  And the truth come tell to me."

4 "It is the bluid of my greyhound,
  Mother lady, mother lady:
 It is the bluid of my greyhound,
  And it wadna rin for me."

5 "Hound's bluid was neer sae red,
  Son Davie, son Davie:
 Hound's bluid was neer sae red,
  And the truth come tell to me."

6 "It is the bluid o' my brither John,
  Mother lady, mother lady,
 It is the bluid o' my brither John,
  And the truth I have told to thee."

7 "What about did the plea begin,
  Son Davie, son Davie?"
 "It began about the cutting of a willow wand
  That would never been a tree."

8 "What death dost thou desire to die,
  Son Davie, son Davie?
 What death dost thou desire to die?
  And the truth come tell to me."

9 "I'll set my foot in a bottomless ship,
  Mother lady, mother lady:
 I'll set my foot in a bottomless ship,
  And ye'll never see mair o' me."

10 "What wilt thou leave to thy poor wife,
        Son Davie, son Davie?"
    "Grief and sorrow all her life,
        And she'll never see mair o' me."

11 "What wilt thou leave to thy old son,
        Son Davie, son Davie?"
    "I'll leave him the weary world to wander up and down,
        And he'll never get mair o' me."

12 "What wilt thou leave to thy mother dear,
        Son Davie, son Davie?"
    "A fire o' coals to burn her, wi' hearty cheer,
        And she'll never get mair o' me."

(B)

1 "Why dois your brand sae drap wi bluid,
                    Edward, Edward,
   Why dois your brand sae drap wi bluid,
       And why sae sàd gang yee O?"
   "O I hae killed my hauke sae guid,
                    Mither, mither,
   O I hae killed my hauke sae guid,
       And I had nae mair bot hee O."

2 "Your haukis bluid was nevir sae reid,
                    Edward, Edward,
   Your haukis bluid was nevir sae reid,
       My deir son I tell thee O."
   "O I hae killed my reid-roan steid,
                    Mither, mither,
   O I hae killed my reid-roan steid,
       That erst was sae fair and frie O."

3 "Your steid was auld, and ye hae gat mair,
                    Edward, Edward,
   Your steid was auld, and ye hae gat mair,
       Sum other dule ye drie O."
   "O I hae killed my fadir deir,
                    Mither, mither,
   O I hae killed my fadir deir,
       Alas, and wae is mee O!" *false climax*

4 "And whatten penance wul ye drie for that,
                Edward, Edward?
And whatten penance will ye drie for that?
  My deir son, now tell me O."
"Ile set my feit in yonder boat,
                Mither, mither,
Ile set my feit in yonder boat,
  And Ile fare ovir the sea O."

5 "And what wul ye doe wi your towirs and your ha,
                Edward, Edward?
And what wul ye doe wi your towirs and your ha,
  That were sae fair to see O?"
"Ile let thame stand tul they doun fa,
                Mither, mither,
Ile let thame stand tul they doun fa,
  For here nevir mair maun I bee O."

6 "And what wul ye leive to your bairns and your wife,
                Edward, Edward?
And what wul ye leive to your bairns and your wife,
  Whan ye gang ovir the sea O?"
"The warldis room, late them beg thrae life,
                Mither, mither,
The warldis room, late them beg thrae life,
  For thame nevir mair wul I see O."

7 "And what wul ye leive to your ain mither deir,
                Edward, Edward?
And what wul ye leive to your ain mither deir?
  My deir son, now tell me O."
"The curse of hell frae me sall ye beir,
                Mither, mither,
The curse of hell frae me sall ye beir,
  Sic counseils ye gave to me O."

Climax

8

Lord Ingram and Chiel Wyet

Child 66 A; Coffin, p. 71

As do most versions of "Edward," this ballad deals with
fratricide, in this case double, but the cause is altogether
more convincing than a difference of opinion over arboricul-
ture. Lord Ingram shows an unusual degree of magnanimity
in a difficult situation, and although we have a predisposition
to sympathize with lovers separated by an arranged marriage,
there is something satisfying in the gratitude which Lady
Maisery, though mad, to be sure, ultimately expresses to
her brief husband. Although it was once reported that "Lord
Ingram" had been found in North America, there is no
further trace of the text.

1   Lord Ingram and Chiel Wyet
         Was baith born in one bower;
     Laid baith their hearts on one lady,
         The less was their honour.

2   Chiel Wyet and Lord Ingram
         Was baith born in one hall;
     Laid baith their hearts on one lady,
         The worse did them befall.

3   Lord Ingram wood her Lady Maisery
         From father and from mother;
     Lord Ingram wood her Lady Maisery
         From sister and from brother.

4   Lord Ingram wood her Lady Maisery
         With leave of a' her kin;
     And every one gave full consent,
         But she said no to him.

5   Lord Ingram wood her Lady Maisery
        Into her father's ha;
    Chiel Wyet wood her Lady Maisery
        Amang the sheets so sma.

6   Now it fell out upon a day,
        She was dressing her head,
    That ben did come her father dear,
        Wearing the gold so red.

7   He said, "Get up now, Lady Maisery,
        Put on your wedding gown;
    For Lord Ingram he will be here,
        Your wedding must be done."

8   "I'd rather be Chiel Wyet's wife,
        The white fish for to sell,
    Before I were Lord Ingram's wife,
        To wear the silk so well.

9   "I'd rather be Chiel Wyet's wife,
        With him to beg my bread,
    Before I were Lord Ingram's wife,
        To wear the gold so red.

10   "Where will I get a bonny boy,
        Will win gold to his fee,
    And will run unto Chiel Wyet's
        With this letter from me?"

11   "O here I am," the boy says,
        "Will win gold to my fee,
    And carry away any letter
        To Chiel Wyet from thee."

12   And when he found the bridges broke,
        He bent his bow and swam;
    And when he found the grass growing,
        He hastened and he ran.

13   And when he came to Chiel Wyet's castle,
        He did not knock nor call,

But set his bent bow to his breast,
    And lightly leaped the wall;
And ere the porter opend the gate,
    The boy was in the hall.

14   The first line that he looked on,
        A grieved man was he;
    The next line that he looked on,
        A tear blinded his ee:
    Says, "I wonder what ails my one brother
        He'll not let my love be!

15   "But I'll send to my brother's bridal—
        The bacon shall be mine—
    Full four and twenty buck and roe,
        And ten tun of the wine;
    And bid my love be blythe and glad,
        And I will follow syne."

16   There was not a groom about that castle
        But got a gown of green,
    And all was blythe, and all was glad,
        But Lady Maisery she was neen.

17   There was no cook about that kitchen
        But got a gown of gray,
    And all was blythe, and all was glad,
        But Lady Maisery was wae.

18   Between Mary Kirk and that castle
        Was all spread ower with garl,
    To keep Lady Maisery and her maidens
        From tramping on the marl.

19   From Mary Kirk to that castle
        Was spread a cloth of gold,
    To keep Lady Maisery and her maidens
        From treading on the mold.

20   When mass was sung, and bells was rung,
        And all men bound for bed,
    Then Lord Ingram and Lady Maisery
        In one bed they were laid.

21 When they were laid into their bed—
        It was baith saft and warm—
    He laid his hand over her side,
        Says, "I think you are with bairn."

22 "I told you once, so did I twice,
        When ye came me to woo,
    That Chiel Wyet, your only brother,
        One night lay in my bower.

23 "I told you twice, so did I thrice,
        Ere ye came me to wed,
    That Chiel Wyet, your one brother,
        One night lay in my bed."

24 "O will you father your bairn on me,
        And on no other man?
    And I'll give him to his dowry
        Full fifty ploughs of land."

25 "I will not father my bairn on you,
        Nor on no wrongeous man,
    Though ye would give him to his dowry
        Five thousand ploughs of land."

26 Then up did start him Chiel Wyet,
        Shed by his yellow hair,
    And gave Lord Ingram to the heart
        A deep wound and a sair.

27 Then up did start him Lord Ingram,
        Shed by his yellow hair,
    And gave Chiel Wyet to the heart
        A deep wound and a sair.

28 There was no pity for that two lords,
        Where they were lying slain;
    But all was for Lady Maisery,
        In that bower she gaed brain.

29 There was no pity for that two lords,
        When they were lying dead;

But all was for her Lady Maisery,
    In that bower she went mad.

30   Said, "Get to me a cloak of cloth,
        A staff of good hard tree;
     If I have been an evil woman,
        I shall beg till I dee.

31   "For a bit I'll beg for Chiel Wyet,
        For Lord Ingram I'll beg three;
     All for the good and honorable marriage
        At Mary Kirk [he] gave me."

9

The Twa Sisters

Child 10 B; Coffin, pp. 38-42

"The Twa Sisters" shows that in the world of ballads sorori-
cide as well as fratricide can spring from frustrated love. In
several versions the younger sister is alive when she reaches
the mill-dam and is killed for her jewelry by the ungentle
miller. Although this addition may soften the elder sister's
crime a little, she is usually burned at a stake hard by the
gallows where the miller hangs. The North American texts
lack the supernatural element of the talking harp constructed
from some part of the heroine's body.

1   There was twa sisters in a bowr,
        Edinburgh, Edinburgh
    There was twa sisters in a bowr,
        Stirling for ay
    There was twa sisters in a bowr,
    There came a knight to be their wooer.
        Bonny Saint Johnston stands upon Tay

2   He courted the eldest wi glove and ring,
     But he lovd the youngest above a' thing.

3   He courted the eldest wi brotch an knife,
     But lovd the youngest as his life.

4   The eldest she was vexed sair,
     An much envi'd her sister fair.

5   Into her bowr she could not rest,
     Wi grief an spite she almos brast.

6   Upon a morning fair an clear,
     She cried upon her sister dear:

7   "O sister, come to yon sea stran,
     An see our father's ships come to lan."

8   She's taen her by the milk-white han,
     An led her down to yon sea stran.

9   The youngest stood upon a stane,
     The eldest came an threw her in.

10   She tooke her by the middle sma,
     An dashd her bonny back to the jaw.

11   "O sister, sister, tak my han,
     An Ise mack you heir to a' my lan.

12   "O sister, sister, tak my middle,
     An yes get my goud and my gouden girdle.

13   "O sister, sister, save my life,
     An I swear Ise never be nae man's wife."

14   "Foul fa the han that I should tacke,
     It twin'd me an my wardles make.

15   "Your cherry cheeks an yallow hair
     Gars me gae maiden for evermair."

16 Sometimes she sank, an sometimes she swam,
    Till she came down yon bonny mill-dam.

17 O out it came the miller's son,
    An saw the fair maid swimmin in.

18 "O father, father, draw your dam,
    Here's either a mermaid or a swan."

19 The miller quickly drew the dam,
    An there he found a drownd woman.

20 You coudna see her yallow hair
    For gold and pearle that were so rare.

21 You coudna see her middle sma
    For gouden girdle that was sae braw.

22 You coudna see her fingers white,
    For gouden rings that was sae gryte.

23 An by there came a harper fine,
    That harped to the king at dine.

24 When he did look that lady upon,
    He sighd and made a heavy moan.

25 He's taen three locks o her yallow hair,
    An wi them strung his harp sae fair.

26 The first tune he did play and sing,
    Was, "Farewell to my father the king."

27 The nextin tune that he playd syne,
    Was, "Farewell to my mother the queen."

28 The lasten tune that he playd then,
    Was, "Wae to my sister, fair Ellen."

10

The Braes O' Yarrow

Child 214 E; Coffin, pp. 129-31

Here a family quarrel, arising from an envious brother's distaste at the size of his sister's dowry, results in much bloodshed and sorrow. The villain appears to emerge unscathed and in prospect of repossessing the livestock, but one suspects that he had better eat with caution in Sarah's house. Some North American versions suggest derivation from print rather than from tradition.

1 Late at een, drinkin the wine,
  Or early in a mornin,
The set a combat them between,
  To fight it in the dawnin.

2 "O stay at hame, my noble lord!
  O stay at hame, my marrow!
My cruel brother will you betray,
  On the dowy houms o Yarrow."

3 "O fare ye weel, my lady gaye!
  O fare ye weel, my Sarah!
For I maun gae, tho I neer return
  Frae the dowy banks o Yarrow."

4 She kissd his cheek, she kaimed his hair,
  As she had done before, O;
She belted on his noble brand,
  An he's awa to Yarrow.

5 O he's gane up yon high, high hill—
  I wat he gaed wi sorrow—
An in a den spied nine armd men,
  I the dowy houms o Yarrow.

6 "O ir ye come to drink the wine,
    As ye hae doon before, O?
  Or ir ye come to wield the brand,
    On the bonny banks o Yarrow?"

7 "I im no come to drink the wine,
    As I hae doon before, O,
  But I im come to wield the brand,
    On the dowy houms o Yarrow."

8 Four he hurt, an five he slew,
    On the dowy houms o Yarrow,
  Till that stubborn knight came him behind,
    An ran his body thorrow.

9 "Gae hame, gae hame, good-brother John,
    An tell your sister Sarah
  To come an lift her noble lord,
    Who's sleepin sound on Yarrow."

10 "Yestreen I dreamd a dolefu dream;
    I kend there wad be sorrow;
  I dreamd I pu'd the heather green,
    On the dowy banks o Yarrow."

11 She gaed up yon high, high hill—
    I wat she gaed wi sorrow—
  An in a den spy'd nine dead men,
    On the dowy houms o Yarrow.

12 She kissd his cheek, she kaimd his hair,
    As oft she did before, O;
  She drank the red blood frae him ran,
    On the dowy houms o Yarrow.

13 "O haud your tongue, my douchter dear,
    For what needs a' this sorrow?
  I'll wed you on a better lord
    Than him you lost on Yarrow."

14 "O haud your tongue, my father dear,
    An dinna grieve your Sarah;

A better lord was never born
Than him I lost on Yarrow.

15 "Tak hame your ousen, take hame your kye,
    For they hae bred our sorrow;
I wiss that they had a' gane mad
    Whan they cam first to Yarrow."

11

Lord Randal

Child 12 A; Coffin, pp. 42-5

"Lord Randal" shares with "Edward" and other ballads the method of narrative development by dialogue, and here, as in "Edward," the speakers are mother and son. There is less suspense, however, and the hero's reason for bequeathing hell and fire is more immediately obvious. In some versions the eels are boiled in broth, made into a pie, or fried in butter; again the hero reports having eaten fish, often speckled fish with white bellies, and, at least once, a little four-footed fish. We are to assume that Lord Randal had dined on snakes (one American version has "rattle and eel broth," and another "fried eels and a serpent") or lizards, though sometimes he knows that he had a cup of strong poison for breakfast. The poisoner is usually a sweetheart, but occasionally a stepmother, grandmother, wife, sister, or grandpa, a combination of two of the above, or even the dying man himself. In no case apparently does a British or American version give a motive for the murder, but this is not an uncommon ballad omission. "Lord Randal" has been one of the most widespread and popular of the Child ballads in North America.

couplets

1 "O where ha you been, Lord Randal, my son?
    And where ha you been, my handsome young man?"
"I ha been at the greenwood; mother, mak my bed soon,
    For I'm wearied wi hunting, and fain wad lie down."

2   "An wha met ye there, Lord Randal, my son?
     An wha met you there, my handsome young man?"
     "O I met wi my true-love; mother, mak my bed soon,
     For I'm wearied wi hunting, and fain wad lie down."

3   "And what did she give you, Lord Randal, my son?
     And what did she give you, my handsome young man?"
     "Eels fried in a pan; mother, mak my bed soon,
     For I'm wearied wi huntin, and fain wad lie down."

4   "An wha gat your leavins, Lord Randal, my son?
     And wha gat your leavins, my handsome young man?"
     "My hawks and my hounds; mother, mak my bed soon,
     For I'm wearied wi huntin, and fain wad lie down."

5   "And what becam of them, Lord Randal, my son?
     And what becam of them, my handsome young man?"
     "They stretched their legs out and died; mother, mak my
         bed soon,
     For I'm wearied wi huntin, and fain wad lie down."

6   "O I fear you are poisoned, Lord Randal, my son!
     I fear you are poisoned, my handsome young man!"
     "O yes, I am poisoned; mother, mak my bed soon,
     For I'm sick at the heart, and I fain wad lie down."

7   "What d'ye leave to your mother, Lord Randal, my son?
     What d'ye leave to your mother, my handsome young
         man?"
     "Four and twenty milk kye; mother, mak my bed soon,
     For I'm sick at the heart, and I fain wad lie down."

8   "What d'ye leave to your sister, Lord Randal, my son?
     What d'ye leave to your sister, my handsome young
         man?"
     "My gold and my silver; mother, mak my bed soon,
     For I'm sick at the heart, an I fain wad lie down."

9   "What d'ye leave to your brother, Lord Randal, my son?
     What d'ye leave to your brother, my handsome young
         man?"

"My houses and my lands; mother, mak my bed soon,
For I'm sick at the heart, and I fain wad lie down."

10   "What d'ye leave to your true-love, Lord Randal, my son?
What d'ye leave to your true-love, my handsome young
        man?"
"I leave her hell and fire; mother, mak my bed soon,
For I'm sick at the heart, and I fain wad lie down."

12

Bonny Barbara Allan

Child 84 A; Coffin, pp. 87-90

Once more a lady brings about her lover's death, though
Barbara does not have to resort to such drastic means as did
Lord Randal's lady. We find some grounds advanced for Barbara's hardheartedness, but they scarcely justify her action, or
lack of it, nor need there be such justification. Pepys enjoyed
the ballad, but some of his pleasure may have come from its
singer, the actress Mrs. Knepp, for whom he had an interest
which he concealed neither from his *Diary* nor from the lady.
They exchanged notes, she signing herself Barbary Allen, and
he, somewhat more revealingly, Dapper Dicky. One need not
read between the lines of the *Diary* to assert that no young
man need have died for the hardness of Mrs. Knepp's heart
or hand. Mrs. Pepys's reaction to the ballad has not been preserved, but we know what she thought of Mrs. Knepp. "Barbara Allan" made Goldsmith cry, and as he heard it from an
old dairymaid we may be fairly sure that it was the poem
alone which moved him. Probably no Child ballad has been
found more often on this side of the Atlantic. For a special
study see Joseph W. Hendren, "Bonny Barbara Allen," *Folk
Travelers*, etc., Publication of the Texas Folklore Society,
XXV, 1953, pp. 47-74.

1 It was in and about the Martinmas time,
    When the green leaves were a falling,
  That Sir John Græme, in the West Country,
    Fell in love with Barbara Allan.

2 He sent his man down through the town,
    To the place where she was dwelling:
  "O haste and come to my master dear,
    Gin ye be Barbara Allan."

3 O hooly, hooly rose she up,
    To the place where he was lying,
  And when she drew the curtain by,
    "Young man, I think you're dying."

4 "O it's I'm sick, and very, very sick,
    And 't is a' for Barbara Allan:"
  "O the better for me ye's never be,
    Tho your heart's blood were a spilling.

5 "O dinna ye mind, young man," said she,
    "When ye was in the tavern a drinking,
  That ye made the healths gae round and round,
    And slighted Barbara Allan?"

6 He turnd his face unto the wall,
    And death was with him dealing:
  "Adieu, adieu, my dear friends all,
    And be kind to Barbara Allan."

7 And slowly, slowly raise she up,
    And slowly, slowly left him,
  And sighing said, she could not stay,
    Since death of life had reft him.

8 She had not gane a mile but twa,
    When she heard the dead-bell ringing,
  And every jow that the dead-bell geid,
    It cry'd, "Woe to Barbara Allan!"

9 "O mother, mother, make my bed!
      O make it saft and narrow!
   Since my love died for me to-day,
      I'll die for him to-morrow."

13

The Douglas Tragedy

(Earl Brand)

Child 7 B; Coffin, pp. 35-7

Lady Margaret represents the ballad heroine at her best.
She has an imperturbable love and faith which falter only
when she sees her father about to be killed. For a moment
she expresses the truism that a lover is easier to replace than
a father, but once she has performed the customary filial duties to a dying parent she rides on with Lord William and
responds to his death with the only appropriate gesture, her
own. The rose and briar growing from the lovers' graves to
intertwine are an appealing ballad convention with a fairly
obvious animistic source; see Wimberley, *Folklore in the English and Scottish Ballads,* pp. 38-41. Behind "The Douglas
Tragedy" lies an old continental story better represented in
other Child versions which are more faithful but less poetic
than the one given here. North American versions are common.

1 "Rise up, rise up, now, Lord Douglas," she says,
      "And put on your armour so bright;
   Let it never be said that a daughter of thine
      Was married to a lord under night.

2 "Rise up, rise up, my seven bold sons,
      And put on your armour so bright,
   And take better care of your youngest sister,
      For your eldest's awa the last night."

3   He's mounted her on a milk-white steed,
     And himself on a dapple grey,
With a bugelet horn hung down by his side,
     And lightly they rode away.

4   Lord William lookit oer his left shoulder,
     To see what he could see,
And there he spy'd her seven brethren bold,
     Come riding over the lee.

5   "Light down, light down, Lady Margret," he said,
     "And hold my steed in your hand,
Until that against your seven brethren bold,
     And your father, I mak a stand."

6   She held his steed in her milk-white hand,
     And never shed one tear,
Until that she saw her seven brethren fa,
     And her father hard fighting, who lovd her so dear.

7   "O hold your hand, Lord William!" she said,
     "For your strokes they are wondrous sair;
True lovers I can get many a ane,
     But a father I can never get mair."

8   O she's taen out her handkerchief,
     It was o the holland sae fine,
And aye she dighted her father's bloody wounds,
     That were redder than the wine.

9   "O chuse, O chuse, Lady Margret," he said,
     "O whether will ye gang or bide?"
"I'll gang, I'll gang, Lord William," she said,
     "For ye have left me no other guide."

10   He's lifted her on a milk-white steed,
     And himself on a dapple grey,
With a bugelet horn hung down by his side
     And slowly they baith rade away.

11   O they rade on, and on they rade,
     And a' by the light of the moon,

Until they came to yon wan water,
And there they lighted down.

12 They lighted down to tak a drink
    Of the spring that ran sae clear,
    And down the stream ran his gude heart's blood,
    And sair she gan to fear.

13 "Hold up, hold up, Lord William," she says,
    "For I fear that you are slain;"
    " 'Tis naething but the shadow of my scarlet cloak,
    That shines in the water sae plain."

14 O they rade on, and on they rade,
    And a' by the light of the moon,
    Until they cam to his mother's ha door,
    And there they lighted down.

15 "Get up, get up, lady mother," he says,
    "Get up, and let me in!
    Get up, get up, lady mother," he says,
    "For this night my fair lady I've win.

16 "O mak my bed, lady mother," he says,
    "O mak it braid and deep,
    And lay Lady Margret close at my back,
    And the sounder I will sleep."

17 Lord William was dead lang ere midnight,
    Lady Margret lang ere day,
    And all true lovers that go thegither,
    May they have mair luck than they!

18 Lord William was buried in St. Mary's kirk,
    Lady Margret in Mary's quire;
    Out o the lady's grave grew a bonny red rose,
    And out o the knight's a briar.

19 And they twa met, and they twa plat,
    And fain they wad be near;
    And a' the warld might ken right weel
    They were twa lovers dear.

20 But bye and rade the Black Douglas,
    And wow but he was rough!
For he pulld up the bonny brier,
    And flang 't in St. Mary's Loch.

14

Fair Janet

Child 64 A

There is an apparent gap between stanzas 10 and 11, but
this may indicate a transition not unusually abrupt for ballad
style rather than a delicate distaste to describe childbirth.
The ballad muse prefers sylvan parturition, where the mother
can set her back against a thorn, thus emulating, with a difference, the nightingale of poetic tradition. "Fair Janet" has
not as yet been found in North America.

1   "Ye maun gang to your father, Janet,
    Ye maun gang to him soon;
  Ye maun gang to your father, Janet,
    In case that his days are dune."

2   Janet's awa to her father,
    As fast as she could hie:
  "O what's your will wi me, father?
    O what's your will wi me?"

3   "My will wi you, Fair Janet," he said,
    "It is both bed and board;
  Some say that ye loe Sweet Willie,
    But ye maun wed a French lord."

4   "A French lord maun I wed, father?
    A French lord maun I wed?
  Then, by my sooth," quo Fair Janet,
    "He's neer enter my bed."

5   Janet, awa to her chamber,
        As fast as she could go;
    Wha's the first ane that tapped there,
        But Sweet Willie her jo?

6   "O we maun part this love, Willie,
        That has been lang between;
    There's a French lord coming oer the sea,
        To wed me wi a ring;
    There's a French lord coming oer the sea,
        To wed and tak me hame."

7   "If we maun part this love, Janet,
        It causeth mickle woe;
    If we maun part this love, Janet,
        It makes me into mourning go."

8   "But ye maun gang to your three sisters,
        Meg, Marion, and Jean;
    Tell them to come to Fair Janet,
        In case that her days are dune."

9   Willie's awa to his three sisters,
        Meg, Marion, and Jean:
    "O haste, and gang to Fair Janet,
        I fear that her days are dune."

10 Some drew to them their silken hose,
        Some drew to them their shoon.
    Some drew to them their silk manteils,
        Their coverings to put on,
    And they're awa to Fair Janet,
        By the hie light o the moon.

                *   *   *

11 "O I have born this babe, Willie,
        Wi mickle toil and pain;
    Take hame, take hame, your babe, Willie,
        For nurse I dare be nane."

12 He's tane his young son in his arms,
        And kisst him cheek and chin,

And he's awa to his mother's bower,
   By the hie light o the moon.

.3 "Open, open, mother," he says,
   "O open and let me in;
The rain rains on my yellow hair,
   And the dew drops oer my chin,
And I hae my young son in my arms,
   I fear that his days are dune."

14 With her fingers lang and sma
   She lifted up the pin,
And with her arms long and sma
   Received the baby in.

15 "Gae back, gae back now, Sweet Willie,
   And comfort your fair lady;
For where ye had but ae nourice,
   Your young son shall hae three."

16 Willie he was scarce awa,
   And the lady put to bed,
Whan in and came her father dear:
   "Make haste, and busk the bride."

17 "There's a sair pain in my head, father,
   There's a sair pain in my side;
And ill, O ill, am I, father,
   This day for to be a bride."

18 "O ye maun busk this bonny bride,
   And put a gay mantle on;
For she shall wed this auld French lord,
   Gin she should die the morn."

19 Some pat on the gay green robes,
   And some pat on the brown;
But Janet put on the scarlet robes,
   To shine foremost throw the town.

20 And some they mounted the black steed,
   And some mounted the brown;

But Janet mounted the milk-white steed,
To ride foremost throw the town.

21 "O wha will guide your horse Janet?
O wha will guide him best?"
"O wha but Willie, my true-love?
He kens I loe him best."

22 And whan they cam to Marie's kirk,
To tye the haly ban,
Fair Janet's cheek looked pale and wan,
And her colour gaed an cam.

23 When dinner it was past and done,
And dancing to begin,
"O we'll go take the bride's maidens,
And we'll go fill the ring."

24 O ben there cam the auld French lord,
Saying, "Bride, will ye dance with me?"
"Awa, awa, ye auld French lord,
Your face I downa see."

25 O ben than cam now Sweet Willie,
He cam with ane advance:
"O I'll go tak the bride's maidens,
And we'll go tak a dance."

26 "I've seen ither days wi you, Willie,
And so has mony mae,
Ye would hae danced wi me mysel,
Let a' my maidens gae."

27 O ben than cam now Sweet Willie,
Saying, "Bride, will ye dance wi me?"
"Aye, by my sooth, and that I will,
Gin my back should break in three."

28 She had nae turned her throw the dance,
Throw the dance but thrice,
Whan she fell doun at Willie's feet,
And up did never rise.

29 Willie's taen the key of his coffer,
   And gien it to his man:
 "Gae hame, and tell my mother dear
   My horse he has me slain;
 Bid her be kind to my young son,
   For father he has nane."

30 The tane was buried in Marie's kirk,
   And the tither in Marie's quire;
 Out of the tane there grew a birk,
   And of the tither a bonny brier.

15

Lord Thomas and Fair Annet

Child 73 A; Coffin, pp. 74-6

Even though Mr. Child called this version "one of the most
beautiful of our ballads, and indeed of all ballads," we may
have trouble in taking Lord Thomas as an ideal hero and
lover. He vacillates between beauty and property, and at the
testing time property wins. Then most inopportunely he seems
to change again, and the result is two murders and a suicide.
One may even confess an unorthodox sympathy for the nut-
brown bride: after all she had not asked Lord Thomas to
marry her property or Fair Annet to come to the wedding.
"Lord Thomas" has been extremely popular in North America.

1 Lord Thomas and Fair Annet
   Sate a' day on a hill;
 Whan night was cum, and sun was sett,
   They had not talkt their fill.

2 Lord Thomas said a word in jest,
   Fair Annet took it ill:
 "A, I will nevir wed a wife
   Against my ain friends' will."

3   "Gif ye wull nevir wed a wife,
        A wife wull neir wed yee:"
      Sae he is hame to tell his mither,
        And knelt upon his knee.

4   "O rede, O rede, mither," he says,
        "A gude rede gie to mee;
      O sall I tak the nut-browne bride,
        And let Faire Annet bee?"

5   "The nut-browne bride haes gowd and gear,
        Fair Annet she has gat nane;
      And the little beauty Fair Annet haes
        O it wull soon be gane."

6   And he has till his brother gane;
        "Now, brother, rede ye mee;
      A, sall I marrie the nut-browne bride,
        And let Fair Annet bee?"

7   "The nut-browne bride has oxen, brother,
        The nut-browne bride has kye;
      I wad hae ye marrie the nut-browne bride,
        And cast Fair Annet bye."

8   "Her oxen may dye i the house, billie,
        And her kye into the byre,
      And I sall hae nothing to mysell
        Bot a fat fadge by the fyre."

9   And he has till his sister gane:
        "Now, sister, rede ye mee;
      O sall I marrie the nut-browne bride,
        And set Fair Annet free?"

10   "I'se rede ye tak Fair Annet, Thomas,
        And let the browne bride alane;
      Lest ye sould sigh, and say, 'Alace,
        What is this we brought hame!'"

11   "No, I will tak my mither's counsel,
        And marrie me owt o hand;

And I will tak the nut-browne bride,
　　Fair Annet may leive the land."

12　Up then rose Fair Annet's father,
　　　Twa hours or it wer day,
　　And he is gane into the bower
　　　Wherein Fair Annet lay.

13　"Rise up, rise up, Fair Annet," he says,
　　　"Put on your silken sheene;
　　Let us gae to St Marie's kirke,
　　　And see that rich weddeen."

14　"My maides, gae to my dressing-roome,
　　　And dress to me my hair;
　　Whaireir yee laid a plait before,
　　　See yee lay ten times mair.

15　"My maids, gae to my dressing-room,
　　　And dress to me my smock;
　　The one half is o the holland fine,
　　　The other o needle-work."

16　The horse Fair Annet rade upon,
　　　He amblit like the wind;
　　Wi siller he was shod before,
　　　Wi burning gowd behind.

17　Four and twenty siller bells
　　　Wer a' tyed till his mane,
　　And yae tift o the norland wind,
　　　They tinkled ane by ane.

18　Four and twenty gay gude knichts
　　　Rade by Fair Annet's side,
　　And four and twenty fair ladies,
　　　As gin she had bin a bride.

19　And whan she cam to Marie's kirk,
　　　She sat on Marie's stean:
　　The cleading that Fair Annet had on
　　　It skinkled in their een.

20   And whan she cam into the kirk,
        She shimmerd like the sun;
    The belt that was about her waist
        Was a' wi pearles bedone.

21   She sat her by the nut-browne bride,
        And her een they wer sae clear,
    Lord Thomas he clean forgat the bride,
        Whan Fair Annet drew near.

22   He had a rose into his hand,
        He gae it kisses three,
    And reaching by the nut-browne bride,
        Laid it on Fair Annet's knee.

23   Up than spak the nut-browne bride,
        She spak wi meikle spite:
    "And whair gat ye that rose-water,
        That does mak yee sae white?"

24   "O I did get the rose-water
        Whair ye wull neir get nane,
    For I did get that very rose-water
        Into my mither's wame."

25   The bride she drew a long bodkin
        Frae out her gay head-gear,
    And strake Fair Annet unto the heart,
        That word spak nevir mair.

26   Lord Thomas he saw Fair Annet wex pale,
        And marvelit what mote bee;
    But whan he saw her dear heart's blude,
        A' wood-wroth wexed hee.

27   He drew his dagger, that was sae sharp,
        That was sae sharp and meet,
    And drave it into the nut-browne bride,
        That fell deid at his feit.

28   "Now stay for me, dear Annet," he sed,
        "Now stay, my dear," he cry'd;

Then strake the dagger untill his heart,
　　And fell deid by her side.

29　Lord Thomas was buried without kirk-wa,
　　　Fair Annet within the quiere,
　　And o the tane thair grew a birk,
　　　The other a bonny briere.

30　And ay they grew, and ay they threw,
　　　As they wad faine be neare;
　　And by this ye may ken right weil
　　　They were twa luvers deare.

16

Glasgerion

Child 67 A

Whatever the age of the ballad, its harper hero is at least older than Chaucer's *House of Fame* where he is listed with such eminent musicians as Orpheus and Arion. He also appears in Gavin Douglas's *Palace of Honour*, but this may be no more than an echo of Chaucer. The aristocratic belief that a churl's son can never be other than churlish is effectively illustrated by Jack's sorry behaviour. A captious critic might object that Glasgerion went to sleep more readily and slept more soundly than the circumstances seemed to demand.

1　Glasgerion was a kings owne sonne,
　　　And a harper he was good;
　　He harped in the kings chamber,
　　　Where cuppe and candle stoode,
　　And soe did hee in the queens chamber,
　　　Till ladies waxed wood.

2　And then bespake the kings daughter,
　　　And these words thus sayd shee:

. . . .
. . . .

3   Saide, "Strike on, strike on, Glasgerrion,
        Of thy striking doe not blinne;
    There's never a stroke comes over thin harpe
        But it glads my hart within."

4   "Faire might you fall, lady!" quoth hee;
        "Who taught you now to speake?
    I have loved you, lady, seven yeere;
        My hart I durst neere breake."

5   "But come to my bower, my Glasgerryon,
        When all men are att rest;
    As I am a ladie true of my promise,
        Thou shalt bee a welcome guest."

6   But hom then came Glasgerryon,
        A glad man, Lord, was hee:
    "And come thou hither, Jacke, my boy,
        Come hither unto mee.

7   "For the kings daughter of Normandye,
        Her love is granted mee,
    And beffore the cocke have crowen,
        Att her chamber must I bee."

8   "But come you hither, master," quoth hee,
        "Lay your head downe on this stone;
    For I will waken you, master deere,
        Afore it be time to gone."

9   But upp then rose that lither ladd,
        And did on hose and shoone;
    A collar he cast upon his necke;
        Hee seemed a gentleman.

10 And when he came to that ladies chamber,
        He thrild upon a pinn;
    The lady was true of her promise,
        Rose up and lett him in.

11 He did not take the lady gay
   To boulster nor to bedd,
But downe upon her chamber-flore
   Full soone he hath her layd.

12 He did not kisse that lady gay
   When he came nor when he youd;
And sore mistrusted that lady gay
   He was of some churlës blood.

13 But home then came that lither ladd,
   And did of his hose and shoone,
And cast that coller from about his necke;
   He was but a churlës sonne:
"Awaken," quoth hee, "my master deere,
   I hold it time to be gone."

14 "For I have sadled your horsse, master,
   Well bridled I have your steed;
Have not I served a good breakfast,
   When time comes I have need."

15 But up then rose good Glasgerryon,
   And did on both hose and shoone,
And cast a coller about his necke;
   He was a kingës sonne.

16 And when he came to that ladies chamber,
   He thrild upon a pinn;
The lady was more than true of promise,
   Rose up and let him in.

17 Saies, "Whether have you left with me
   Your braclett or your glove?
Or are you returned backe againe
   To know more of my love?"

18 Glasgerryon swore a full great othe,
   By oake and ashe and thorne,
"Lady, I was never in your chamber
   Sith the time that I was borne."

19 "O then it was your litle foote-page
     Falsly hath beguiled me:"
   And then shee pulld forth a litle pen-kniffe,
     That hanged by her knee,
   Says, "There shall never noe churlës blood
     Spring within my body.

20 But home then went Glasgerryon,
     A woe man, good [Lord], was hee;
   Sayes, "Come hither, thou Jacke, my boy,
     Come thou hither to me.

21 "For if I had killed a man to-night,
     Jacke, I wold tell it thee;
   But if I have not killed a man to-night,
     Jacke, thou hast killed three!"

22 And he pulld out his bright browne sword,
     And dryed it on his sleeve,
   And he smote off that lither ladds head,
     And asked noe man noe leave.

23 He sett the swords poynt till his brest,
     The pumill till a stone;
   Thorrow that falsenese of that lither ladd
     These three lives werne all gone.

17

Little Musgrave

Child 81 A; Coffin, pp. 84-6

There are many resemblances between this ballad and "Old
Robin of Portingale," which immediately precedes it in Child,
but there are differences as well. Lady Bernard is merely unfaithful to her husband, while Old Robin's wife plots to murder him in addition, and whereas Lord Bernard kills only the

adulterous pair, Old Robin disposed of twenty-four other good knights. Even if the reader is surprised by Lord Bernard's somewhat melodramatic repentance, he cannot fail to be affected by his scrupulous regard for the respect due to good birth. In North America the hero frequently appears as Little Matthy Groves, or some variant of that name.

1   As it fell one holy-day,
        Hay downe
    As many be in the yeare,
    When young men and maids together did goe,
        Their mattins and masse to heare,

2   Little Musgrave came to the church-dore;
        The preist was at private masse;
    But he had more minde of the faire women
        Then he had of Our Lady's grace.

3   The one of them was clad in green,
        Another was clad in pall,
    And then came in my lord Bernard's wife,
        The fairest amonst them all.

4   She cast an eye on Little Musgrave,
        As bright as the summer sun;
    And then bethought this Little Musgrave,
        This lady's heart have I woonn.

5   Quoth she, "I have loved thee, Little Musgrave,
        Full long and many a day;"
    "So have I loved you, fair lady,
        Yet never word durst I say."

6   "I have a bower at Buckelsfordbery,
        Full daintyly it is deight;
    If thou wilt wend thither, thou Little Musgrave,
        Thou's lig in mine armes all night."

7   Quoth he, "I thank yee, faire lady,
        This kindnes thou showest to me;
    But whether it be to my weal or woe,
        This night I will lig with thee."

8 With that he heard, a little tynë page,
      By his ladye's coach as he ran:
   "All though I am my ladye's foot-page,
      Yet I am Lord Barnard's man.

9 "My lord Barnard shall knowe of this,
      Whether I sink or swim;"
   And ever where the bridges were broake
      He laid him downe to swimme.

10 "A sleepe or wake, thou Lord Barnard,
       As thou art a man of life,
   For Little Musgrave is at Bucklesfordbery,
       A bed with thy own wedded wife."

11 "If this be true, thou little tinny page,
       This thing thou tellest to me,
   Then all the land in Bucklesfordbery
       I freely will give to thee.

12 "But if it be a ly, thou little tinny page,
       This thing thou tellest to me,
   On the hyest tree in Bucklesfordbery
       Then hanged shalt thou be."

13 He called up his merry men all:
       "Come saddle me my steed;
   This night must I to Buckellsfordbery,
       For I never had greater need."

14 And some of them whistld, and some of them sung,
       And some these words did say,
   And ever when my lord Barnard's horn blew,
       "Away, Musgrave, away!"

15 "Methinks I hear the thresel-cock,
       Methinks I hear the jaye;
   Methinks I hear my lord Barnard,
       And I would I were away."

16 "Lye still, lye still, thou Little Musgrave,
       And huggell me from the cold;

'Tis nothing but a shephard's boy,
   A driving his sheep to the fold.

17 "Is not thy hawke upon a perch?
     Thy steed eats oats and hay;
   And thou a fair lady in thine armes,
     And wouldst thou bee away?"

18 With that my lord Barnard came to the dore,
     And lit a stone upon;
   He plucked out three silver keys,
     And he opend the dores each one.

19 He lifted up the coverlett,
     He lifted up the sheet:
   "How now, how now, thou Littell Musgrave,
     Doest thou find my lady sweet?"

20 "I find her sweet," quoth Little Musgrave,
     "The more 't is to my paine;
   I would gladly give three hundred pounds
     That I were on yonder plaine."

21 "Arise, arise, thou Littell Musgrave,
     And put thy clothës on;
   It shall nere be said in my country
     I have killed a naked man.

22 "I have two swords in one scabberd,
     Full deere they cost my purse;
   And thou shalt have the best of them,
     And I will have the worse."

23 The first stroke that Little Musgrave stroke,
     He hurt Lord Barnard sore;
   The next stroke that Lord Barnard stroke,
     Little Musgrave nere struck more.

24 With that bespake this faire lady,
     In bed whereas she lay:
   "Although thou'rt dead, thou Little Musgrave,
     Yet I for thee will pray.

25   "And wish well to thy soule will I,
        So long as I have life;
    So will I not for thee, Barnard,
        Although I am thy wedded wife."

26   He cut her paps from off her brest;
        Great pitty it was to see
    That some drops of this ladie's heart's blood
        Ran trickling downe her knee.

27   "Woe worth you, woe worth, my mery men all,
        You were nere borne for my good;
    Why did you not offer to stay my hand,
        When you see me wax so wood?

28   "For I have slaine the bravest sir knight
        That ever rode on steed;
    So have I done the fairest lady
        That ever did woman's deed.

29   "A grave, a grave," Lord Barnard cryd,
        "To put these lovers in;
    But lay my lady on the upper hand,
        For she came of the better kin."

18

Bonnie James (George) Campbell

Child 210 A and C; Coffin, p. 128

It has often been observed that there is but slight narrative element in this touching song, two versions of which are given, and critics have usually been content to call it along with "The Bonny Earl of Murray" (24) a coronach, threnody, or lament. Whatever we name it, the poem, even incomplete as in the first version, or perhaps improved as in the second, has the magic touch of effective pathos. The ballad has not been common in North America.

(A)

1   O it's up in the Highlands,
     And along the sweet Tay,
  Did bonie James Campbell
     Ride monie a day.

2   Sadled and bridled,
     And bonie rode he;
  Hame came horse, hame came sadle,
     But neer hame cam he.

3   And doun cam his sweet sisters,
     Greeting sae sair,
  And down cam his bonie wife,
     Tearing her hair.

4   "My house is unbigged,
     My barn's unbeen,
  My corn's unshorn,
     My meadow grows green."

(C)

1   Hie upon Hielands,
     And laigh upon Tay,
  Bonnie George Campbell
     Rode out on a day.

2   He saddled, he bridled,
     And gallant rode he,
  And hame cam his guid horse,
     But never cam he.

3   Out cam his mother dear,
     Greeting fu sair,
  And out cam his bonnie bryde,
     Riving her hair.

4   "The meadow lies green,
     The corn is unshorn,
  But bonnie George Campbell
     Will never return."

5   Saddled and bridled
     And booted rode he,
    A plume in his helmet,
     A sword at his knee.

6   But toom cam his saddle,
     All bloody to see,
    Oh, hame cam his guid horse,
     But never cam he!

19

Lamkin

Child 93 A; Coffin, pp. 94-6

"Lamkin" is unusual among ballads in its grim portrayal of class struggle. When Lord Wearie, the impoverished and improvident aristocrat who must have a new castle whether he can afford it or not, leaves the country rather than sell his lands and pay his mason, the embittered craftsman's wrongs drive him to irrationality and murder. His accomplice, equally disgruntled, though for less apparent reason, is more ruthless than Lamkin himself. There are few more ghoulish and gruesome scenes in the ballads, or even in children's fairy tales, than that in which Lamkin rocks the cradle and the nurse sings as the bonny babe's blood runs out of the cradle and down to the hall floor. "Lamkin" has been widespread in North America.

1   It's Lamkin was a mason good
     As ever built wi stane;
    He build Lord Wearie's castle,
     But payment got he nane.

2   "O pay me Lord Wearie,
     Come, pay me my fee:
    "I canna pay you, Lamkin,
     For I maun gang oer the sea."

3 "O pay me now, Lord Wearie,
    Come, pay me out o hand:"
  "I canna pay you, Lamkin,
    Unless I sell my land."

4 "O gin ye winna pay me,
    I here sall mak a vow,
  Before that ye come hame again,
    Ye sall hae cause to rue."

5 Lord Wearie got a bonny ship,
    To sail the saut sea faem;
  Bade his lady weel the castle keep,
    Ay till he should come hame.

6 But the nourice was a fause limmer
    As eer hung on a tree;
  She laid a plot wi Lamkin,
    Whan her lord was oer the sea.

7 She laid a plot wi Lamkin,
    Whan the servants were awa,
  Loot him in at a little shot-window,
    And brought him to the ha.

8 "O whare's a' the men o this house,
    That ca me Lamkin?"
  "They're at the barn-well thrashing;
    'T will be lang ere they come in."

9 "And whare's the women o this house,
    That ca me Lamkin?"
  "They're at the far well washing;
    'T will be lang ere they come in."

10 "And whare's the bairns o this house,
    That ca me Lamkin?"
  "They're at the school reading;
    'T will be night or they come hame."

11 "O whare's the lady o this house,
    That ca's me Lamkin?"

"She's up in her bower sewing,
    But we soon can bring her down."

12   Then Lamkin's tane a sharp knife,
        That hang down by his gaire,
    And he has gien the bonny babe
        A deep wound and a sair.

13   Then Lamkin he rocked,
        And the fause nourice sang,
    Till frae ilkae bore o the cradle
        The red blood out sprang.

14   Then out it spak the lady,
        As she stood on the stair:
    "What ails my bairn, nourice,
        That he's greeting sae sair?

15   "O still my bairn, nourice,
        O still him wi the pap!"
    "He winna still, lady,
        For this nor for that."

16   "O still my bairn, nourice,
        O still him wi the wand!"
    "He winna still, lady,
        For a' his father's land."

17   "O still my bairn, nourice,
        O still him wi the bell!"
    "He winna still, lady,
        Till ye come down yoursel."

18   O the firsten step she steppit,
        She steppit on a stane;
    But the neisten step she steppit,
        She met him Lamkin.

19   "O mercy, mercy, Lamkin,
        Hae mercy upon me!
    Though you've taen my young son's life,
        Ye may let mysel be."

20 "O sall I kill her, nourice,
        Or sall I lat her be?"
    "O kill her, kill her, Lamkin,
        For she neer was good to me."

21 "O scour the bason, nourice,
        And mak it fair and clean,
    For to keep this lady's heart's blood,
        For she's come o noble kin."

22 "There need nae bason, Lamkin,
        Lat it run through the floor;
    What better is the heart's blood
        O the rich than o the poor?"

23 But ere three months were at an end,
        Lord Wearie came again;
    But dowie, dowie was his heart
        When first he came hame.

24 "O wha's blood is this," he says,
        "That lies in the chamer?"
    "It is your lady's heart's blood;
        'T is as clear as the lamer."

25 "And wha's blood is this," he says,
        "That lies in my ha?"
    "It is your young son's heart's blood;
        'T is the clearest ava."

26 O sweetly sang the black-bird
        That sat upon the tree;
    But sairer grat Lamkin,
        When he was condemnd to die.

27 And bonny sang the mavis,
        Out o the thorny brake;
    But sairer grat the nourice,
        When she was tied to the stake.

HISTORICAL BALLADS

❧

20

Sir Patrick Spens

Child 58 A; Coffin, p. 68

To call a ballad historical must suggest that it has the appearance rather than the reality of history; as Mr. Child said of the present ballad, "A strict accordance with history should not be expected, and indeed would be almost a ground of suspicion." Three historical events, respectively of 1281, 1290, and 1589, have been suggested with varying degrees of assurance as inspiring the ballad, but no one of these has received general acceptance. The version given here, the earliest to be printed, is found in Percy's *Reliques* and of its source Percy says only that it is "given from two MS. copies transmitted from Scotland." One of these copies would appear to be from David Dalrymple, Lord Hailes, and the other probably from John McGowan; see *The Correspondence of Thomas Percy and David Dalrymple, Lord Hailes,* edited by A. F. Falconer, Louisiana State University Press, 1954, pp. 39, 48, n1, 50, and, in another connection, pp. 155-6. Except in the unlikely event that the two manuscripts were identical, our version must owe something to Percy's editorial hand. If so, the hand was less clumsy and obvious than elsewhere, and even Ritson reprinted the ballad from the *Reliques* with virtually no changes and without adverse comments on the text. Although fairly common in Great Britain it has been very rare in North America, where only two versions appear to have been recorded. Among the songs of Jack Chase, an English-born sailor in Melville's *White Jacket,* was "Sir Patrick Spens was the best sailor that ever sailed the sea."

1 The king sits in Dumferling toune,
   Drinking the blude-reid wine:
"O whar will I get guid sailor,
   To sail this schip of mine?"

2 Up and spak an eldern knicht,
   Sat at the kings richt kne:
"Sir Patrick Spence is the best sailor
   That sails upon the se."

3 The king has written a braid letter,
   And signd it wi his hand,
And sent it to Sir Patrick Spence,
   Was walking on the sand.

4 The first line that Sir Patrick red,
   A loud lauch lauched he;
The next line that Sir Patrick red,
   The teir blinded his ee.

5 "O wha is this has don this deid,
   This ill deid don to me,
To send me out this time o' the yeir,
   To sail upon the se!

6 "Mak hast, mak haste, my mirry men all,
   Our guid schip sails the morne:"
"O say na sae, my master deir,
   For I feir a deadlie storme.

7 "Late late yestreen I saw the new moone,
   Wi the auld moone in hir arme,
And I feir, I feir, my deir master,
   That we will cum to harme."

8 O our Scots nobles wer richt laith
   To weet their cork-heild schoone;
Bot lang owre a' the play wer playd,
   Their hats they swam aboone.

9 O lang, lang may their ladies sit,
   Wi thair fans into their hand,

Or eir they se Sir Patrick Spence
    Cum sailing to the land.

10   O lang, lang may the ladies stand,
    Wi thair gold kems in their hair,
  Waiting for thair ain deir lords,
    For they'll se thame na mair.

11   Haf owre, haf owre to Aberdour,
    It's fiftie fadom deip,
  And thair lies guid Sir Patrick Spence,
    Wi the Scots lords at his feit.

21

The Hunting of the Cheviot

Child 162 A; Coffin, pp. 112-3

"The Hunting of the Cheviot," often known as "Chevy Chase," is the second of two ballads related distantly to each other and treating with great freedom a common theme, the Battle of Otterburn, August 19, 1388. Although the first of these, "The Battle of Otterburn" (Child 161), represents an earlier stage, no copy of it is as old as our version of the "Hunting." We do not know how soon after the battle the original poem or poems were composed, but both are listed in The Complaynt of Scotland (1549), and it was in one form or another of this poem that the ballad may be said to have been introduced to the critics. Sir Philip Sidney's words in the Defence of Poesy are too well known not to be quoted once more: "Certeinly I must confesse mine owne barbarousnesse, I never heard the old Song of Percy and Duglas, that I found not my heart mooved more then with a Trumpet: and yet is it sung but by some blinde Crowder, with no rougher voyce, then rude stile: which being so evill apparelled in the dust and Cobwebbes of that uncivil age, what would it worke, trimmed in the gorgious

eloquence of *Pindare*? In *Hungarie* I have seene it the manner of all Feastes, and other such meetings, to have songs
of their ancestors valure, which that right soldierlike nation,
think one of the cheifest kindlers of brave courage." When
Addison devoted numbers 70 and 74 of the *Spectator* (1711)
to praise of "the old song of 'Chevy Chase'," we know that
he was reading the late and inferior broadside version
(Child B). Some contemporary critics derided Addison's
taste, but one fears that they would have thought no more
of the older version. Addison says that "Ben Jonson used
to say that he had rather have been the author of it than of
all his works," a remark not otherwise recorded, though
Jonson did say to Drummond that if he had written Southwell's "Burning Babe" "he would have been content to
destroy many of his." It is hardly likely that Addison's statement could have been a distortion of this, because though a
selection from the *Conversations with Drummond* was pub-
lished in 1711, it did not contain the passage on Southwell.
There is less doubt about Dr. Johnson's opinion of the ballad.
In 1784 he is quoted by William Windham as saying, "Chevy
Chase pleased the vulgar, but did not satisfy the learned; it
did not fill a mind capable of thinking strongly." The versions found in North America are shortened forms of Child B.

1 The Persë owt off Northombarlonde,
       And a vowe to God mayd he
   That he wold hunte in the mowntayns
       Off Chyviat within days thre,
   In the magger of doughtë Dogles,
       And all that ever with him be.

2 The fattiste hartes in all Cheviat
       He sayd he wold kyll, and cary them away:
   "Be my feth," sayd the dougheti Doglas agayn,
       "I wyll let that hontyng yf that I may."

3 Then the Persë owt off Banborowe cam,
       With him a myghtee meany,
   With fifteen hondrith archares bold off blood and bone;
       The wear chosen owt of shyars thre.

4 This begane on a Monday at morn,
       In Cheviat the hyllys so he;

The chylde may rue that ys un-born,
   It wos the mor pittë.

5   The dryvars thorowe the woodës went,
     For to reas the dear;
   Bomen byckarte uppone the bent
     With ther browd aros cleare.

6   Then the wyld thorowe the woodës went,
     On every sydë shear;
   Greahondes thorowe the grevis glent,
     For to kyll thear dear.

7   This begane in Chyviat the hyls abone,
     Yerly on a Monnyn-day;
   Be that it drewe to the oware off none,
     A hondrith fat hartës ded ther lay.

8   The blewe a mort uppone the bent,
     The semblyde on sydis shear;
   To the quyrry then the Persë went,
     To se the bryttlynge off the deare.

9   He sayd, "It was the Doglas promys
     This day to met me hear;
   But I wyste he wolde faylle, verament;"
     A great oth the Persë swear.

10 At the laste a squyar off Northomberlonde
     Lokyde at his hand full ny;
   He was war a the doughetie Doglas commynge,
     With him a myghttë meany.

11 Both with spear, bylle, and brande,
     Yt was a myghtti sight to se;
   Hardyar men, both off hart nor hande,
     Wear not in Cristiantë.

12 The wear twenti hondrith spear-men good,
     Withoute any feale;
   The wear borne along be the watter a Twyde,
     Yth bowndës of Tividale.

13 "Leave of the brytlyng of the dear," he sayd,
    "And to your boÿs lock ye tayk good hede;
For never sithe ye wear on your mothars borne
    Had ye never so mickle nede."

14 The dougheti Dogglas on a stede,
    He rode alle his men beforne;
His armor glytteryde as dyd a glede;
    A boldar barne was never born.

15 "Tell me whos men ye ar," he says,
    "Or whos men that ye be:
Who gave youe leave to hunte in this Chyviat chays,
    In the spyt of myn and of me."

16 The first mane that ever him an answear mayd,
    Yt was the good lord Persë:
"We wyll not tell the whoys men we ar," he says,
    "Nor whos men that we be;
But we wyll hounte hear in this chays,
    In the spyt of thyne and of the.

17 "The fattiste hartës in all Chyviat
    We have kyld, and cast to carry them away:"
"Be my troth," sayd the dougletë Dogglas agayn,
    "Therfor the ton of us shall de this day."

18 Then sayd the doughtë Doglas
    Unto the lord Persë:
"To kyll alle thes giltles men,
    Alas, it wear great pittë!

19 "But, Persë, thowe art a lord of lande,
    I am a yerle callyd within my contrë;
Let all our men uppone a parti stande,
    And do the battell off the and of me."

20 "Nowe Cristes cors on his crowne," sayd the lorde Persë,
    "Who-so-ever ther-to says nay!
Be my troth, doughttë Doglas," he says,
    "Thou shalt never se that day.

21 "Nethar in Ynglonde, Skottlonde, nar France,
       Nor for no man of a woman born,
   But, and fortune be my chance,
       I dar met him, on man for on."

22 Then bespayke a squyar off Northombarlonde,
       Richard Wytharyngton was his nam;
   "It shall never be told in Sothe-Ynglonde," he says,
       "To Kyng Herry the Fourth for sham.

23 "I wat youe byn great lordës twaw,
       I am a poor squyar of lande;
   I wylle never se my captayne fyght on a fylde,
   `   And stande my selffe and loocke on,
   But whylle I may my weppone welde,
       I wylle not [fayle] both hart and hande."

24 That day, that day, that dredfull day!
       The first fit here I fynde;
   And youe wyll here any mor a the hountynge a the
       Chyviat,
       Yet ys ther mor behynde.

25 The Yngglyshe men hade ther bowys yebent,
       Ther hartes wer good yenoughe;
   The first off arros that the shote off,
       Seven skore spear-men the sloughe.

26 Yet byddys the yerle Doglas uppon the bent,
       A captayne good yenoughe,
   And that was sene verament,
       For he wrought hom both woo and wouche.

27 The Dogglas partyd his ost in thre,
       Lyk a cheffe cheften off pryde;
   With suar spears off myghttë tre,
       The cum in on every syde;

28 Thrughe our Yngglyshe archery
       Gave many a wounde fulle wyde;
   Many a doughetë the garde to dy,
       Which ganyde them no pryde.

29   The Ynglyshe men let ther boÿs be,
         And pulde owt brandes that wer brighte;
      It was a hevy syght to se
         Bryght swordes on basnites lyght.

30   Thorowe ryche male and myneyeple,
         Many sterne the strocke done streght;
      Many a freyke that was fulle fre,
         Ther under foot dyd lyght.

31   At last the Duglas and the Persë met,
         Lyk to captayns of myght and of mayne;
      The swapte togethar tylle the both swat,
         With swordes that wear of fyn myllan.

32   Thes worthë freckys for to fyght,
         Ther-to the wear fulle fayne,
      Tylle the bloode owte off thear basnetes sprente,
         As ever dyd heal or rayn.

33   "Yelde the, Persë," sayde the Doglas,
         "And i feth I shalle the brynge
      Wher thowe shalte have a yerls wagis
         Of Jamy our Skottish kynge.

34   "Thou shalte have thy ransom fre,
         I hight the hear this thinge;
      For the manfullyste man yet art thowe
         That ever I conqueryd in filde fighttynge."

35   "Nay," sayd the lord Persë,
         "I told it the beforne,
      That I wolde never yeldyde be
         To no man of a woman born."

36   With that ther cam an arrowe hastely,
         Forthe off a myghttë wane;
      Hit hathe strekene the yerle Duglas
         In at the brest-bane.

37   Thorowe lyvar and longës bathe
         The sharpe arrowe ys gane,

That never after in all his lyffe-days
    He spayke mo wordës but ane:
That was, "Fyghte ye, my myrry men, whyllys ye may,
    For my lyff-days ben gan."

38   The Persë leanyde on his brande,
    And sawe the Duglas de;
   He tooke the dede mane by the hande,
    And sayd, "Wo ys me for the!"

39   "To have savyde thy lyffe, I wolde have partyde with
    My landes for years thre,
   For a better man, of hart nare of hande,
    Was nat in all the north contrë."

40   Off all that se a Skottishe knyght,
    Was callyd Ser Hewe the Monggombyrry;
   He sawe the Duglas to the deth was dyght,
    He spendyd a spear, a trusti tre.

41   He rod uppone a corsiare·
    Throughe a hondrith archery:
   He never stynttyde, nar never blane,
    Tylle he cam to the good lord Persë.

42   He set uppone the lorde Persë
    A dynte that was full soare;
   With a suar spear of a myghttë tre
    Clean thorow the body he the Persë ber,

43   A the tothar syde that a man myght se
    A large cloth-yard and mare:
   Towe bettar captayns wear nat in Cristiantë
    Then that day slan wear ther.

44   An archar off Northomberlonde
    Say slean was the lord Persë;
   He bar a bende bowe in his hand,
    Was made off trusti tre.

45   An arow that a cloth-yarde was lang
    To the harde stele halyde he;

A dynt that was both sad and soar
  He sat on Ser Hewe the Monggombyrry.

46 The dynt yt was both sad and sar
      That he of Monggomberry sete;
    The swane-fethars that his arrowe bar
      With his hart-blood the wear wete.

47 Ther was never a freake wone foot wolde fle,
      But still in stour dyd stand,
    Heawyng on yche othar, whylle the myghte dre,
      With many a balfull brande.

48 This battell begane in Chyviat
      An owar befor the none,
    And when even-songe bell was rang,
      The battell was nat half done.

49 The tocke . . . on ethar hande
      Be the lyght off the mone;
    Many hade no strenght for to stande,
      In Chyviat the hillys abon.

50 Of fifteen hondrith archars of Ynglonde
      Went away but seventi and thre;
    Of twenti hondrith spear-men of Skotlonde,
      But even five and fifti.

51 But all wear slayne Cheviat within;
      The hade no strengthe to stand on hy;
    The chylde may rue that ys unborne,
      It was the mor pittë.

52 Thear was slayne, withe the lord Persë,
      Ser Johan of Agerstone,
    Ser Rogar, the hinde Hartly,
      Ser Wyllyam, the bolde Hearone.

53 Ser Jorg, the worthë Loumle,
      A knyghte of great renowen,
    Ser Raff, the ryche Rugbe,
      With dyntes wear beaten dowene.

54 For Wetharryngton my harte was wo,
        That ever he slayne shulde be;
    For when both his leggis wear hewyne in to,
        Yet he knyled and fought on hys kny.

55 Ther was slayne, with the dougheti Duglas,
        Ser Hewe the Monggombyrry,
    Ser Davy Lwdale, that worthë was,
        His sistars son was he.

56 Ser Charls a Murre in that place,
        That never a foot wolde fle;
    Ser Hewe Maxwelle, a lorde he was,
        With the Doglas dyd he dey.

57 So on the morrowe the mayde them byears
        Off birch and hasell so gray;
    Many wedous, with wepying tears,
        Cam to fache ther makys away.

58 Tivydale may carpe off care,
        Northombarlond may mayk great mon,
    For towe such captayns as slayne wear thear
        On the March-parti shall never be non.

59 Word ys commen to Eddenburrowe,
        To Jamy the Skottishe kynge,
    That dougheti Duglas, lyff-tenant of the Marches,
        He lay slean Chyviot within.

60 His handdës dyd he weal and wryng,
        He sayd, "Alas, and woe ys me!
    Such an othar captayn Skotland within,"
        He sayd, "ye-feth shuld never be."

61 Worde ys commyn to lovly Londone,
        Till the fourth Harry our kynge,
    That lord Persë, leyff-tenante of the Marchis,
        He lay slayne Chyviat within.

62 "God have merci on his solle," sayde Kyng Harry,
        "Good lord, yf thy will it be!

I have a hondrith captayns in Ynglonde," he sayd,
  "As good as ever was he:
But, Persë, and I brook my lyffe,
  Thy deth well quyte shall be."

63 As our noble kynge mayd his avowe,
    Lyke a noble prince of renowen,
For the deth of the lord Persë
    He dyde the battell of Hombylldown;

64 Wher syx and thrittë Skottishe knyghtes
    On a day wear beaten down;
Glendale glytteryde on ther armor bryght,
    Over castille, towar, and town.

65 This was the hontynge off the Cheviat,
    That tear begane this spurn;
Old men that knowen the grownde well yenoughe
    Call it the battell of Otterburn.

66 At Otterburn begane this spurne,
    Uppone a Monnynday;
Ther was the doughtë Doglas slean,
    The Persë never went away.

67 Ther was never a tym on the Marchepartës
    Sen the Doglas and the Persë met,
But yt ys mervele and the rede blude ronne not,
    As the reane doys in the stret.

68 Jhesue Crist our balys bete,
    And to the blys us brynge!
Thus was the hountynge of the Chivyat:
    God send us alle good endyng!

22

Johnie Armstrong

Child 169 A

This ballad is better history than most; indeed the account in the ballad is so close to that given in Robert Lindesay of Pitscottie's *Historie and Chronicles of Scotland* (to 1575) as to suggest that one derives from the other. Pitscottie's dates are uncertain, but as they are sometimes given as *c.* 1532 to *c.* 1578, and as there is a reference to "iohonne ermistrangis dance" in *The Complaynt of Scotland* (1549), it is probable that the ballad came first and that Pitscottie, like other chroniclers, did not hesitate on occasion to draw upon popular ballads for material not otherwise available. It is, of course, possible that the dance tune is quite distinct from the ballad and merely another proof of Johnie's fame. Johnie, a member of a large and unruly family in Liddesdale which pillaged impartially on both sides of the border, was first mentioned in 1525 and was summarily executed in 1530 when James V was engaged in discouraging organized thievery and rapine along his turbulent borders. Although Johnie's death may not have been precisely as related here, there seems little doubt from the other records that his capture was accomplished by means of ill faith. That our version is English in more than language is indicated by its placing Johnie in Westmorland and the subsequent reference to Scots as false, an adjective almost proverbial in this context in northern England. "Johnny Armstrong," along with "Chevy Chase," was known by the milk-woman and her daughter in Walton's *Complete Angler*.

1   There dwelt a man in faire Westmerland,
    Jonnë Armestrong men did him call,
  He had nither lands nor rents coming in,
    Yet he kept eight score men in his hall.

2   He had horse and harness for them all,
        Goodly steeds were all milke-white;
    O the golden bands an about their necks,
        And their weapons, they were all alike.

3   Newes then was brought unto the king
        That there was a sicke a won as hee,
    That livëd lyke a bold out-law,
        And robbëd all the north country.

4   The king he writt an a letter then,
        A letter which was large and long;
    He signëd it with his owne hand,
        And he promised to doe him no wrong.

5   When this letter came Jonnë untill,
        His heart it was as blythe as birds on the tree:
    "Never was I sent for before any king,
        My father, my grandfather, nor none but mee.

6   "And if wee goe the king before,
        I would we went most orderly;
    Every man of you shall have his scarlet cloak,
        Laced with silver laces three.

7   "Every won of you shall have his velvett coat,
        Laced with silver lace so white;
    O the golden bands an about your necks,
        Black hatts, white feathers, all alyke."

8   By the morrow morninge at ten of the clock,
        Towards Edenburough gon was hee,
    And with him all his eight score men;
        Good lord, it was a goodly sight for to see!

9   When Jonnë came befower the king,
        He fell downe on his knee;
    "O pardon, my soveraine leige," he said,
        "O pardon my eight score men and mee!"

10 "Thou shalt have no pardon, thou traytor strong,
        For thy eight score men nor thee;

For to-morrow morning by ten of the clock,
    Both thou and them shall hang on the gallow-tree."

11   But Jonnë looke'd over his left shoulder,
        Good Lord, what a grevious look looked hee!
    Saying, "Asking grace of a graceless face—
        Why there is none for you nor me."

12   But Jonnë had a bright sword by his side,
        And it was made of the mettle so free,
    That had not the king stept his foot aside,
        He had smitten his head from his faire boddë.

13   Saying, "Fight on, my merry men all,
        And see that none of you be taine;
    For rather then men shall say we were hange'd,
        Let them report how we were slaine."

14   Then, God wott, faire Eddenburrough rose,
        And so besett poore Jonnë rounde,
    That fowerscore and tenn of Jonnës best men
        Lay gasping all upon the ground.

15   Then like a mad man Jonnë laide about,
        And like a mad man then fought hee,
    Untill a falce Scot came Jonnë behinde,
        And runn him through the faire boddee.

16   Saying, "Fight on, my merry men all,
        And see that none of you be taine;
    For I will stand by and bleed but awhile,
        And then will I come and fight againe."

17   Newes then was brought to young Jonnë **Armestrong**,
        As he stood by his nurses knee,
    Who vowed if ere he live'd for to be a man,
        O the treacherous Scots revengd hee'd be.

23

Mary Hamilton

Child 173 A; Coffin, pp. 116-7

"Mary Hamilton," one of the most moving of ballads, is doubtless historical in origin, but the history is by no means clear or undisputed. The version before us tells a story of adultery, infanticide, and execution at the Scottish court. The principal figures are a maid of honor, Darnley, and Mary Queen of Scots, but there is no evidence that Mary had an attendant gentlewoman named Hamilton nor, despite Darnley's reputation, is he known to have been involved in any such affair as this. On the other hand, in 1563 the queen's apothecary and one of her French maids were hanged for the killing of their illegitimate child. Certainly if this event be the source of the ballad, the changes illustrate the folk's fondness for aristocratic protagonists, though in some versions the seducer is not a king at all and in one (U) he is an apothecary. Difficulty arises not from anything unlikely in the alteration of the story, but from the fact that a girl named Mary Hamilton, maid of honor to Peter the Great's wife, was beheaded in 1719 for the murder of at least three illegitimate children, one of whom may have been fathered by Peter. In any event Peter insisted on the execution, attended it, kissed the lady's severed head, and "made a little discourse on the anatomy of it to the spectators." The coincidence, to say the least, is amazing and Mr. Child was for a time inclined to believe that the ballad, despite its appearance, was late and a very conscious reworking of the Russian story. Andrew Lang (*Blackwood's Magazine,* 1895, pp. 381-90), however, made so convincing a case for the traditional story that Mr. Child was persuaded, as most others have been, though A. H. Tolman argues, not unreasonably, that while the ballad sprang from the scandal of 1563, "many of the texts later became deeply colored by the similar happening at the Russian court" (*Publications of the Modern Language Association,* 42 [1927], 422-32). If this be the case, one would give much to know how the Russian story found its way among the ballad singers. The ballad has been seldom found in North America.

1   Word's gane to the kitchen,
        And word's gane to the ha,
    That Marie Hamilton gangs wi bairn
        To the hichest Stewart of a'.

2   He's courted her in the kitchen,
        He's courted her in the ha,
    He's courted her in the laigh cellar,
        And that was warst of a'.

3   She's tyed it in her apron
        And she's thrown it in the sea;
    Says, "Sink ye, swim ye, bonny wee babe!
        You'l neer get mair o me."

4   Down then cam the auld queen,
        Goud tassels tying her hair:
    "O Marie, where's the bonny wee babe
        That I heard greet sae sair?"

5   "There never was a babe intill my room,
        As little designs to be;
    It was but a touch o my sair side,
        Come oer my fair bodie."

6   "O Marie, put on your robes o black,
        Or else your robes o brown,
    For ye maun gang wi me the night,
        To see fair Edinbro town."

7   "I winna put on my robes o black,
        Nor yet my robes o brown;
    But I'll put on my robes o white,
        To shine through Edinbro town."

8   When she gaed up the Cannogate,
        She laughd loud laughters three;
    But whan she cam down the Cannogate
        The tear blinded her ee.

drop relates to
doom of death

9   When she gaed up the Parliament stair,
        The heel cam aff her shee;
    And lang or she cam down again
        She was condemnd to dee.

10 When she cam down the Cannogate,
        The Cannogate sae free,
    Many a ladie lookd oer her window,
        Weeping for this ladie.

11 "Ye need nae weep for me," she says,
        "Ye need nae weep for me;
    For had I not slain mine own sweet babe,
        This death I wadna dee.

12 "Bring me a bottle of wine," she says,
        "The best that eer ye hae,
    That I may drink to my weil-wishers,
        And they may drink to me.

13 "Here's a health to the jolly sailors,
        That sail upon the main;
    Let them never let on to my father and mother
        But what I'm coming hame.

14 "Here's a health to the jolly sailors,
        That sail upon the sea;
    Let them never let on to my father and mother
        That I cam here to dee.

15 "Oh little did my mother think,
        The day she cradled me,
    What lands I was to travel through,
        What death I was to dee.

16 "Oh little did my father think,
        The day he held up me,
    What lands I was to travel through,
        What death I was to dee.

17 "Last night I washd the queen's feet,
        And gently laid her down;

And a' the thanks I've gotten the nicht
To be hangd in Edinbro town!

18 "Last nicht there was four Maries,
   The nicht there'l be but three;
There was Marie Seton, and Marie Beton,
And Marie Carmichael, and me."

24

The Bonny Earl of Murray

Child 181 A; Coffin, p. 117

In February, 1592, James Stewart, Earl of Murray, was murdered by George Gordon, Earl of Huntly, and his followers. Tradition has it that as Huntly struck a final blow at the dying man's head, Murray said, "You have spoiled a better face than your own." The act was committed under the guise of a royal commission, and although the king disavowed complicity and professed great regret, Huntly was never called to account. The king perhaps was less distressed by the earl's death than by the violent public disapproval, but his enmity to Murray can be more plausibly ascribed to his belief that the earl was a partisan of Francis Stewart, Earl of Bothwell, than, as the ballad says, that he was the queen's lover. The ballad itself is lacking in narrative element and has often been called a threnody and compared to the Gaelic coronachs. The occasional appearance of the ballad in North America seems due to recent importation rather than to tradition.

1 Ye Highlands, and ye Lawlands,
   Oh where have you been?
They have slain the Earl of Murray,
And they layd him on the green.

2   "Now wae be to thee, Huntly!
        And wherefore did you sae?
    I bade you bring him wi you,
        But forbade you him to slay."

3   He was a braw gallant,
        And he rid at the ring:
    And the bonny Earl of Murray,
        Oh he might have been a king!

4   He was a braw gallant,
        And he playd at the ba;
    And the bonny Earl of Murray
        Was the flower amang them a'.

5   He was a braw gallant,
        And he playd at the glove;
    And the bonny Earl of Murray,
        Oh he was the Queen's love!

6   Oh lang will his lady
        Look oer the castle Down,
    Eer she see the Earl of Murray
        Come sounding thro the town!

25

Jock o' the Side

Child 187 A; Coffin, p. 118

Some similarity is obvious in story between "Jock o' the
Side" and "Kinmont Willie," (Child 186) but whereas "Kinmont Willie" is good history but a suspect ballad, "Jock"
is an honest ballad with no clear historical basis. There are
references to a John of the Side in the middle of the sixteenth
century, but no records of any substance. Mr. Child placed
"Jock" after "Kinmont Willie," because "it may be a free version of his story." Perhaps, but such events and adventures

were hardly uncommon in a territory where theft, especially of cattle, was better than respectable, and imprisonment a recognized occupational hazard. Our version, from Bishop Percy's *Folio Manuscript* is slightly imperfect at the beginning, but the story is clear. We may be permitted to wonder what the critical verdicts would have been had the sole copy of "Jock" been that which is printed in the *Minstrelsy of the Scottish Border*. Mr. Child said of "Jock": "The ballad is one of the best in the world, and enough to make a horse-trooper of any young borderer, had he lacked the impulse." In North America only traces of a single version have been found.

* * *

1 Peeter a Whifeild he hath slaine,
   And John a Side, he is tane,
   And John is bound both hand and foote,
   And to the New-castle he is gone.

2 But tydinges came to the Sybill o the Side,
   By the water-side as shee rann;
   Shee tooke her kirtle by the hem,
   And fast shee runn to Mangerton.

3 . . . .
   The lord was sett downe at his meate;
   When these tydings shee did him tell,
   Never a morsell might he eate.

4 But lords, the wrunge their fingars white,
   Ladyes did pull themselves by the haire,
   Crying, "Alas and weladay!
   For John o the Side wee shall never see more.

5 "But wee'le goe sell our droves of kine,
   And after them our oxen sell,
   And after them our troopes of sheepe,
   But wee will loose him out of the New Castell."

6 But then bespake him Hobby Noble,
   And spoke these words wonderous hye;
   Sayes, "Give me five men to my selfe,
   And I'le feitch John o the Side to thee."

7   "Yea, thou'st have five, Hobby Noble,
        Of the best that are in this countrye;
    I'le give thee five thousand, Hobby Noble,
        That walke in Tyvidale trulye."

8   "Nay, I'le have but five," saies Hobby Noble,
        "That shall walke away with mee;
    Wee will ryde like noe men of warr;
        But like poore badgers wee wilbe."

9   They stuffet up all their baggs with straw,
        And their steeds barefoot must bee;
    "Come on, my brethren," sayes Hobby Noble,
        "Come on your wayes, and goe with mee."

10 And when they came to Culerton ford,
        The water was up, they cold it not goe;
    And then they were ware of a good old man,
        How his boy and hee were at the plowe.

11 "But stand you still," sayes Hobby Noble,
        "Stand you still heere at this shore,
    And I will ryde to yonder old man,
        And see where the gate it lyes ore.

12 "But Christ you save, father!" quoth hee,
        "Crist both you save and see!
    Where is the way over this ford?
        For Christ's sake tell itt mee!"

13 "But I have dwelled heere three score yeere,
        Soe have I done three score and three;
    I never sawe man nor horsse goe ore,
        Except itt were a horse of tree."

14 "But fare thou well, thou good old man!
        The devill in hell I leave with thee,
    Noe better comfort heere this night
        Thow gives my brethren heere and me."

15 But when he came to his brether againe,
        And told this tydings full of woe,

And then they found a well good gate
    They might ryde ore by two and two.

16   And when they were come over the forde,
        All safe gotten att the last,
    "Thankes be to God!" sayes Hobby Nobble,
        "The worst of our perill is past."

17   And then they came into Howbrame wood,
        And there then they found a tree,
    And cutt itt downe then by the roote;
        The lenght was thirty foote and three.

18   And four of them did take the planke,
        As light as it had beene a flee,
    And carryed itt to the New Castle,
        Where as John a Side did lye.

19   And some did climbe up by the walls,
        And some did climbe up by the tree,
    Untill they came upp to the top of the castle,
        Where John made his moane trulye.

20   He sayd, "God be with thee, Sybill o the Side!
        My owne mother thou art," quoth hee;
    "If thou knew this night I were here,
        A woe woman then woldest thou bee.

21   "And fare you well, Lord Mangerton!
        And ever I say God be with thee!
    For if you knew this night I were heere,
        You wold sell your land for to loose mee.

22   "And fare thou well, Much, Millers sonne!
        Much, Millars sonne, I say;
    Thou has beene better att merke midnight
        Then ever thou was att noone o the day.

23   "And fare thou well, my good Lord Clough!
        Thou art thy fathers sonne and heire;
    Thou never saw him in all thy liffe
        But with him durst thou breake a speare.

24   "Wee are brothers childer nine or ten.
    And sisters children ten or eleven.
We never came to the feild to fight,
    But the worst of us was counted a man.

25   But then bespake him Hoby Noble,
    And spake these words unto him;
Saies, "Sleepest thou, wakest thou, John o the Side,
    Or art thou this castle within?"

26   "But who is there," quoth John oth Side,
    "That knowes my name soe right and free?"
"I am a bastard-brother of thine;
    This night I am comen for to loose thee."

27   "Now nay, now nay," quoth John o the Side;
    "Itt feares me sore that will not bee;
For a pecke of gold and silver," John sayd,
    "In faith this night will not loose mee."

28   But then bespake him Hobby Noble,
    And till his brother thus sayd hee;
Sayes, "Four shall take this matter in hand,
    And two shall tent our geldings free."

29   Four did breake one dore without,
    Then John brake five himself;
But when they came to the iron dore,
    It smote twelve upon the bell.

30   "Itt feares me sore," sayd Much, the Miller,
    "That heere taken wee all shalbee;"
"But goe away, brethren," sayd John a Side,
    "For ever alas! this will not bee."

31   "But fye upon thee!" sayd Hobby Noble;
    "Much, the Miller, fye upon thee!
It sore feares me," said Hobby Noble,
    "Man that thou wilt never bee."

32   But then he had Flanders files two or three,
    And hee fyled downe that iron dore,

And tooke John out of the New Castle,
    And sayd, "Looke thou never come heere more!"

33 When he had him forth of the New Castle,
     "Away with me, John, thou shalt ryde:"
  But ever alas! itt cold not bee;
     For John cold neither sitt nor stryde.

34 But then he had sheets two or three,
     And bound Johns boults fast to his feete,
  And sett him on a well good steede,
     Himselfe on another by him seete.

35 Then Hobby Noble smiled and loughe,
     And spoke these worde in mickle pryde:
  "Thou sitts soe finely on thy geldinge
     That, John, thou rydes like a bryde."

36 And when they came thorrow Howbrame **towne**,
     Johns horsse there stumbled at a stone;
  "Out and alas!" cryed Much, the Miller,
     "John, thou 'le make us all be tane."

37 "But fye upon thee!" saies Hobby Noble,
     "Much, the Millar, fye on thee!
  I know full well," sayes Hobby Noble,
     "Man that thou wilt never bee."

38 And when the came into Howbrame **wood**,
     He had Flanders files two or three
  To file Johns bolts beside his feete,
     That hee might ryde more easilye.

39 Says, "John, now leape over a steede!"
     And John then hee lope over five:
  "I know well," sayes Hobby Noble,
     "John, thy fello is not alive."

40 Then he brought him home to Mangerton;
     The lord then he was att his meate;
  But when John o the Side he there did see,
     For faine hee cold noe more eate.

- 41 He sayes, "Blest be thou, Hobby Noble,
         That ever thou wast man borne!
      Thou hast feitched us home good John oth Side,
         That was now cleane from us gone.

OUTLAW BALLADS

❧

26

Robin Hood and Guy of Gisborne

Child 118; Coffin, pp. 104-5

In the B version of *Piers Plowman,* usually dated 1377, Sloth, a personification of one of the Seven Deadly Sins, confesses that while he does not know his paternoster perfectly, he does know "rymes of Robyn Hood and Randolf erle of Chestre." Clearly the poet is not commending Sloth's choice, and it may be that "rymes," which surely must mean ballads, is used in the derogatory sense in which Chaucer sometimes uses it. Rimed stories of Robin Hood, then, must have been in existence for a sufficient time before 1377 to make the allusion meaningful. The earl of Chester referred to is probably the Rannulf who held the title between 1181 and 1232, but no ballads about him are known. The precise age of the earliest extant Robin Hood ballads is not certain. Several survive in manuscripts or prints of the fifteenth century, and linguistic evidence suggests that some of these were composed as early as 1400. The bulk, however, are much later and some are popular only in theme. *A Gest of Robyn Hode,* printed toward the end of the fifteenth century, is of extreme importance in that it represents a rough and ready union of three distinct ballads, no one of which exists outside the *Gest.* It may be considered a first step toward the formation of a popular epic and should be read, both for its own sake and for its implications, by all students of the ballad. Only its length (456 stanzas) prevents its appearance in this volume.

Robin Hood, the generous outlaw who steals from the rich and aids the poor and oppressed, has had and continues to have great popular appeal. Ballads about him were composed

early and late, and since Scott's *Ivanhoe* he has made frequent
appearances in historical novels either as hero or in the sup-
porting cast. Outside the ballads themselves Robin's most
poetic appearance is in Keats' "Robin Hood" (1818), written
in response to his friend Reynolds' sonnets on the outlaw.
Later in the same year Keats on his northern trip heard an
old man sing a ballad of "Robin Huid" containing the line
"Before the King you shall go, go, go, before the King you
shall go," which would appear to be "Robin Hood and the
Bishop of Hereford" (Child 144), otherwise known only in
late manuscript or print. Inevitably scholars have tried to find
out more about Robin than there is to know. The mytholo-
gizers, who contributed much to the humor of scholarship
and still have their hardy survivors, made him a decayed
divinity, sometimes Woden (Odin) or, from his appearance
in English May-day folk-drama, a fertility spirit, or a forest
elf. Only slightly more prosaic are the efforts to identify him
as an historical figure, and here a rich profusion of candidates
has been presented ranging freely over several centuries of
English history. Not long ago a former Attorney-General of
England could write that he knew little about his ancestors
except that "Robin Hood is said to have been one of them."
The fact is that the name Robin (Robertus, Robert) Hood
was disconcertingly frequent through the years, and even
when we find a Robin Hood in trouble over the game laws in
1354 we are not quite justified in the belief that we have
definitely caught our outlaw. Mr. Child rejected both mythol-
ogy and history and declared that "Robin Hood is absolutely
a creation of the ballad-muse," and we may well agree, with
the proviso that some happy scholar may yet identify the
hitherto unknown rogue from whose misdeeds the stories and
ballads grew. Poachers and outlaws were common enough,
and others than Robin appear in the ballads. Romantic tales
of outlaws were not restricted to England; a useful compara-
tive study is Joost de Lange's *The Relation and Development
of English and Icelandic Outlaw Traditions* (Haarlem, 1935).
One may also read with interest, if not with complete acceptance of all its conclusions, P. Valentine Harris, *The Truth
About Robin Hood* (London, 1951).

"Robin Hood and Guy of Gisborne" is found in anything
like completion only in Bishop Percy's *Folio Manuscript,* but
a fragment of a play based on the ballad is extant from the

second half of the fifteenth century. Between stanzas 2 and 3 there is a gap in which Robin dreams of being misused by two men. Later he seems to have a knowledge of John's predicament not hitherto revealed in the ballad itself, and although ballad style is often abrupt in transition and laconic in information, it may well be that the ballad has suffered from a careless transmitter. Apart from our text and the play, the only other trace of the ballad is a highly corrupt version, perhaps in truth not a version at all, found in North Carolina. In general, it may be said that the Robin Hood ballads are not often or well represented in North America.

1   When shawes beene sheene, and shradds full fayre,
      And leeves both large and longe,
   Itt is merry, walking in the fayre forrest,
      To heare the small birds songe.

2   The woodweele sang, and wold not cease,
      Amongst the leaves a lyne:
   And it is by two wight yeomen,
      By deare God, that I meane.

            *   *   *

3   "Me thought they did mee beate and binde,
      And tooke my bow mee froe;
   If I bee Robin a-live in this lande,
      I'le be wrocken on both them towe."

4   "Sweavens are swift, master," quoth John,
      "As the wind that blowes ore a hill;
   For if itt be never soe lowde this night,
      To-morrow it may be still."

5   "Buske yee, bowne yee, my merry men all,
      For John shall goe with mee;
   For I'le goe seeke yond wight yeomen
      In greenwood where the bee."

6   Thé cast on their gowne of greene,
      A shooting gone are they,
   Untill they came to the merry greenwood,
      Where they had gladdest bee;

There were the ware of [a] wight yeoman,
   His body leaned to a tree.

7 A sword and a dagger he wore by his side,
      Had beene many a mans bane,
   And he was cladd in his capull-hyde,
      Topp, and tayle, and mayne.

8 "Stand you still, master," quoth Litle John,
      "Under this trusty tree,
   And I will goe to yond wight yeomen,
      To know his meaning trulye."

9 "A, John, by me thou setts noe store,
      And that's a farley thinge;
   How offt send I my men beffore,
      And tarry my-selfe behinde?

10 "It is noe cunning a knave to ken,
      And a man but heare him speake;
   And itt were not for bursting of my bowe,
      John, I wold thy head breake."

11 But often words they breeden bale,
      That parted Robin and John;
   John is gone to Barnesdale,
      The gates he knowes eche one.

12 And when hee came to Barnesdale,
      Great heavinesse there hee hadd;
   He found two of his fellowes
      Were slaine both in a slade,

13 And Scarlett a foote flyinge was,
      Over stockes and stone,
   For the sheriffe with seven score men
      Fast after him is gone.

14 "Yett one shoote I'le shoote," says Litle John,
      "With Crist his might and mayne;
   I'le make yond fellow that flyes soe fast
      To be both glad and faine."

15 John bent up a good viewe bow,
    And fetteled him to shoote;
The bow was made of a tender boughe,
    And fell downe to his foote.

16 "Woe worth thee, wicked wood," sayd Litle John,
    "That ere thou grew on a tree!
For this day thou art my bale,
    My boote when thou shold bee!"

17 This shoote it was but looselye shott,
    The arrowe flew in vaine,
And it mett one of the sheriffes men;
    Good William a Trent was slaine.

18 It had beene better for William a Trent
    To hange upon a gallowe
Then for to lye in the greenwoode,
    There slaine with an arrowe.

19 And it is sayd, when men be mett,
    Six can doe more then three:
And they have tane Litle John,
    And bound him fast to a tree.

20 "Thou shalt be drawen by dale and downe," quoth the
    sheriffe,
    And hanged hye on a hill:"
"But thou may fayle," quoth Litle John,
    "If itt be Christs owne will."

21 Let us leave talking of Litle John,
    For hee is bound fast to a tree,
And talke of Guy and Robin Hood,
    In the green woode where they bee.

22 How these two yeomen together they mett,
    Under the leaves of lyne,
To see what merchandise they made
    Even at that same time.

23 "Good morrow, good fellow," quoth Sir Guy:
    "Good morrow, good fellow," quoth hee;

"Methinkes by this bow thou beares in thy hand,
    A good archer thou seems to bee."

24 "I am wilfull of my way," quoth Sir Guye,
      "And of my morning tyde:"
    "I'le lead thee through the wood," quoth Robin,
      "Good fellow, I'le be thy guide."

25 "I seeke an outlaw," quoth Sir Guye,
      "Men call him Robin Hood;
    I had rather meet with him upon a day
      Then forty pound of golde."

26 "If you tow mett it wold be seene whether were better
      Afore yee did part awaye;
    Let us some other pastime find,
      Good fellow, I thee pray.

27 "Let us some other masteryes make,
      And wee will walke in the woods even;
    Wee may chance meet with Robin Hoode
      Att some unsett steven."

28 They cutt them downe the summer shroggs
      Which grew both under a bryar,
    And sett them three score rood in twinn,
      To shoote the prickes full neare.

29 "Leade on, good fellow," sayd Sir Guye,
      "Lead on, I doe bidd thee:"
    "Nay, by my faith," quoth Robin Hood,
      "The leader thou shalt bee."

30 The first good shoot that Robin ledd
      Did not shoote an inch the pricke froe;
    Guy was an archer good enoughe,
      But he cold neere shoote soe.

31 The second shoote Sir Guy shott,
      He shott within the garlande;
    But Robin Hoode shott it better then hee,
      For he clove the good pricke-wande.

32   "Gods blessing on thy heart!" sayes Guye,
      "Goode fellow, thy shooting is goode;
For an thy hart be as good as thy hands,
      Thou were better then Robin Hood.

33   "Tell me thy name, good fellow," quoth Guy,
      "Under the leaves of lyne:"
"Nay, by my faith," quoth good Robin,
      "Till thou have told me thine."

34   "I dwell by dale and downe," quoth Guye,
      "And I have done many a curst turne;
And he that calles me by my right name
      Calles me Guye of good Gysborne."

35   "My dwelling is in the wood," sayes Robin;
      "By thee I set right nought;
My name is Robin Hood of Barnesdale,
      A fellow thou has long sought."

36   He that had neither beene a kithe nor kin
      Might have seene a full fayre sight,
To see how together these yeomen went,
      With blades both browne and bright.

37   To have seene how these yeomen together fought,
      Two howers of a summers day;
Itt was neither Guy nor Robin Hood
      That fettled them to flye away.

38   Robin was reacheles on a roote,
      And stumbled at that tyde,
And Guy was quicke and nimble withall,
      And hitt him ore the left side.

39   "Ah, deere Lady!" sayd Robin Hoode,
      "Thou art both mother and may!
I thinke it was never mans destinye
      To dye before his day."

40   Robin thought on Our Lady deere,
      And soone leapt up againe,

And thus he came with an awkwarde stroke;
    Good Sir Guy hee has slayne.

41   He tooke Sir Guys head by the hayre,
        And sticked itt on his bowes end:
    "Thou hast beene traytor all thy liffe,
        Which thing must have an ende."

42   Robin pulled forth an Irish kniffe,
        And nicked Sir Guy in the face,
    That hee was never on a woman borne
        Cold tell who Sir Guye was.

43   Saies, "Lye there, lye there, good Sir Guye,
        And with me be not wrothe;
    If thou have had the worse stroakes at my hand,
        Thou shalt have the better cloathe."

44   Robin did off his gowne of greene,
        Sir Guye hee did it throwe;
    And hee put on that capull-hyde,
        That cladd him toppe to toe.

45   "The bowe, the arrowes, and litle horne,
        And with me now I'le beare;
    For now I will goe to Barnesdale,
        To see how my men doe fare."

46   Robin sett Guyes horne to his mouth,
        A lowd blast in it he did blow;
    That beheard the sheriffe of Nottingham,
        As he leaned under a lowe.

47   "Hearken! hearken!" sayd the sheriffe,
        "I heard noe tydings but good;
    For yonder I heare Sir Guyes horne blowe,
        For he hath slaine Robin Hoode.

48   "For yonder I heare Sir Guyes horne blow,
        Itt blowes soe well in tyde,
    For yonder comes that wighty yeoman,
        Cladd in his capull-hyde.

49 Come hither, thou good Sir Guy,
    Aske of me what thou wilt have:"
"I'le none of thy gold," sayes Robin Hood,
    "Nor I'le none of it have.

50 "But now I have slaine the master," he sayd,
    "Let me goe strike the knave;
This is all the reward I aske,
    Nor noe other will I have."

51 "Thou art a madman," said the shiriffe,
    "Thou sholdest have had a knights fee;
Seeing thy asking [hath] beene soe badd,
    Well granted it shall be."

52 But Litle John heard his master speake,
    Well he knew that was his steven;
"Now shall I be loset," quoth Litle John,
    "With Christs might in heaven."

53 But Robin hee hyed him towards Litle John,
    Hee thought hee wold loose him believe;
The sheriffe and all his companye
    Fast after him did drive.

54 "Stand abacke! stand abacke!" sayd Robin;
    "Why draw you mee soe neere?
Itt was never the use in our countrye
    One's shrift another shold heere."

55 But Robin pulled forth an Irysh kniffe,
    And losed John hand and foote,
And gave him Sir Guyes bow in his hand,
    And bade it be his boote.

56 But John tooke Guyes bow in his hand—
    His arrowes were rawstye by the roote—;
The sherriffe saw Litle John draw a bow
    And fettle him to shoote.

57 Towards his house in Nottingham
    He fled full fast away,

And soe did all his companye,
　Not one behind did stay.

58　But he cold neither soe fast goe,
　　Nor away soe fast runn,
But Litle John, with an arrow broade,
　Did cleave his heart in twinn.

27

Robin Hood and the Monk

Child 119

"Robin Hood and the Monk" is taken from a manuscript of about 1450 and does not seem to be found in oral tradition. There is an unfortunate lacuna after the second line of stanza 30 in which the news of Robin's capture is brought to Sherwood. Two things are worthy of note. First, Robin's piety, which is portrayed in other of the ballads but does not seem too characteristic of a hero who next to sheriffs loves to pillage clerics. Second, his ungenerous if human treatment of John, in which we may perhaps see evidence, supported elsewhere in the ballads, of what is called epic degeneration. Mr. Child says of the poem, "Too much could not be said in praise of this ballad, but nothing need be said. It is very perfection in its kind."

1　In somer, when the shawes be sheyne,
　　And leves be large and long,
　Hit is full mery in feyre foreste
　　To here the foulys song:

2　To se the dere draw to the dale,
　　And leve the hilles hee,
　And shadow hem in the levës grene,
　　Under the grene-wode tre.

3   Hit befel on Whitsontide,
        Erly in a May mornyng,
    The son up feyre can shyne,
        And the briddis mery can syng.

4   "This is a mery mornyng," seid Litull John,
        "Be hym that dyed on tre;
    A more mery man then I am one
        Lyves not in Cristiantë.

5   "Pluk up thi hert, my dere mayster,"
        Litull John can sey,
    "And thynk hit is a full fayre tyme
        In a mornyng of May."

6   "Ye, on thyng greves me," seid Robyn,
        "And does my hert mych woo;
    That I may not no solem day
        To mas nor matyns goo.

7   "Hit is a fourtnet and more," seid he,
        Syn I my savyour see;
    To day wil I to Notyngham," seid Robyn,
        "With the myght of mylde Marye."

8   Than spake Moche, the mylner sun,
        Ever more wel hym betyde!
    "Take twelve of thi wyght yemen,
        Well weppnyd, be thi side.
    Such on wolde thi selfe slon,
        That twelve dar not abyde."

9   "Of all my mery men," seid Robyn,
        "Be my feith I wil non have,
    But Litull John shall beyre my bow,
        Til that me list to drawe."

10 "Thou shall beyre thin own," seid Litull Jon,
        "Maister, and I wyl beyre myne,
    And we well shete a peny," seid Litull Jon,
        "Under the grene-wode lyne."

11   "I wil not shete a peny," seyd Robyn Hode,
       "In feith, Litull John, with the,
     But ever for on as thou shetis," seide Robyn,
       "In feith I holde the thre."

12   Thus shet thei forth, these yemen too,
       Bothe at buske and brome,
     Til Litull John wan of his maister
       Five shillings to hose and shone.

13   A ferly strife fel them betwene,
       As they went bi the wey;
     Litull John seid he had won five shillings,
       And Robyn Hode seid schortly nay.

14   With that Robyn Hode lyed Litul Jon,
       And smote hym with his hande;
     Litul Jon waxed wroth therwith,
       And pulled out his bright bronde.

15   "Were thou not my maister," seid Litull John,
       "Thou shuldis by hit ful sore;
     Get the a man wher thou wilt,
       For thou getis me no more."

16   Then Robyn goes to Notyngham,
       Hym selfe mornyng allone,
     And Litull John to mery Scherwode,
       The pathes he knew ilkone.

17   When Robyn came to Notyngham,
       Sertenly withouten layn,
     He prayed to God and myld Mary
       To bryng hym out save agayn.

18   He gos in to Seynt Mary chirch,
       And kneled down before the rode;
     Alle that ever were the church within
       Beheld wel Robyn Hode.

19   Beside hym stod a gret-hedid munke,
       I pray to God woo he be!

Ful sone he knew gode Robyn,
    As sone as he hym se.

20 Out at the durre he ran,
    Ful sone and anon;
  Alle the yatis of Notyngham
    He made to be sparred everychon.

21 "Rise up," he seid, "thou prowde schereff,
    Buske the and make the bowne;
  I have spyed the kynggis felon,
    For sothe he is in this town.

22 "I have spyed the false felon,
    As he stondis at his masse;
  Hit is long of the," seide the munke,
    "And ever he fro us passe.

23 "This traytur name is Robyn Hode,
    Under the grene-wode lynde;
  He robbyt me onys of a hundred pound,
    Hit shalle never out of my mynde."

24 Up then rose this prowde shereff,
    And radly made hym yare;
  Many was the moder son
    To the kyrk with hyn can fare.

25 In at the durres thei throly thrast,
    With staves ful gode wone;
  "Alas, alas!" seid Robyn Hode,
    "Now mysse I Litull John."

26 But Robyn toke out a too-hond sworde,
    That hangit down be his kne;
  Ther as the schereff and his men stode thyckust,
    Thedurwarde wolde he.

27 Thryes thorowout them he ran then,
    For sothe as I yow sey,
  And woundyt mony a moder son,
    And twelve he slew that day.

28   His sworde upon the schireff hed
         Sertanly he brake in too;
      "The smyth that the made," seid Robyn,
         I pray to God wyrke hym woo!

29   "For now am I weppynlesse," seid Robyn,
         "Alasse! agayn my wylle;
      But if I may fle these traytors fro,
         I wot thei wil me kyll."

30   Robyn in to the churchë ran,
         Throout hem everilkon,
      .   .   .   .
      .   .   .   .

31   Sum fel in swonyng as thei were dede,
         And lay stil as any stone;
      Non of theym were in her mynde
         But only Litull Jon.

32   "Let be your rule," seid Litull Jon,
         "For his luf that dyed on tre,
      Ye that shulde be dughty men;
         Het is gret shame to se.

33   "Oure maister has bene hard bystode
         And yet scapyd away;
      Pluk up your hertis, and leve this mone,
         And harkyn what I shal say.

34   "He has servyd Oure Lady many a day,
         And yet wil, securly;
      Therfor I trust in hir specialy
         No wyckud deth shal he dye.

35   "Therefor be glad," seid Litul John,
         "And let this mournyng be;
      And I shal be the munkis gyde,
         With the myght of mylde Mary.

36   .   .   .   .
         "We wel go but we too;
      And I mete hym," seid Litul John,
      .   .   .   .

37   "Loke that ye kepe wel owre tristil-tre,
          Under the levys smale,
      And spare non of this venyson,
          That gose in thys vale."

38   Forthe then went these yemen too,
          Litul John and Moche on fere,
      And lokid on Moch emys hows,
          The hye way lay full nere.

39   Litul John stode at a wyndow in the mornyng,
          And lokid forth at a stage;
      He was war wher the munke came ridyng,
          And with hym a litul page.

40   "Be my feith," seid Litul John to Moch,
          "I can the tel tithyngus gode;
      I se wher the munke cumys rydyng,
          I know hym be his wyde hode."

41   They went in to the way, these yemen bothe,
          As curtes men and hende;
      Thei spyrred tithyngus at the munke,
          As they had bene his frende.

42   "Fro whens come ye?" seid Litull Jon,
          "Tell us tithyngus, I yow pray,
      Off a false owtlay, [callid Robyn Hode,]
          Was takyn yisterday.

43   "He robbyt me and my felowes bothe
          Of twenti marke in serten;
      If that false owtlay be takyn,
          For sothe we wolde be fayn."

44   "So did he me," seid the munke,
          "Of a hundred pound and more;
      I layde furst hande hym apon,
          Ye may thonke me therfore."

45   "I pray God thanke you," seid Litull John,
          "And we wil when we may;

We will go with you, with your leve,
    And bryng yow on your way.

46 "For Robyn Hode hase many a wilde felow,
    I tell you in certen;
If thei wist ye rode this way,
    In feith ye shulde be slayn."

47 As thei went talking be the way,
    The munke and Litull John,
John toke the munkis horse be the hede,
    Ful sone and anon.

48 Johne toke the munkis horse be the hed,
    For sothe as I yow say;
So did Much the litull page,
    For he shulde not scape away.

49 Be the golett of the hode
    John pulled the munke down;
John was nothyng of hym agast,
    He lete hym falle on his crown.

50 Litull John was sore agrevyd,
    And drew owt his swerde in hye;
The munke saw he shulde be ded,
    Lowd mercy can he crye.

51 "He was my maister," seid Litull John,
    "That thou hase browght in bale;
Shalle thou never cum at our kyng,
    For to telle hym tale."

52 John smote of the munkis hed,
    No longer wolde he dwell;
So did Moch the litull page,
    For ferd lest he wolde tell.

53 Ther thei beryed hem bothe,
    In nouther mosse nor lyng,
And Litull John and Much in fere
    Bare the letturs to oure kyng.

54 . . . .
    He knelid down upon his kne:
  "God yow save, my lege lorde,
    Jhesus you save and se!

55 "God yow save, my lege kyng!"
    To speke John was full bolde;
  He gaf hym the letturs in his hond,
    The kyng did hit unfold.

56 The kyng red the letturs anon,
    And seid, "So mot I the,
  Ther was never yoman in mery Inglond
    I longut so sore to se.

57 "Wher is the munke that these shuld have brought?"
    Oure kyng can say:
  "Be my trouth," seid Litull John,
    "He dyed after the way."

58 The kyng gaf Moch and Litul Jon
    Twenti pound in sertan,
  And made theim yemen of the crown,
    And bade theim go agayn.

59 He gaf John the seel in hand,
    The sheref for to bere,
  To bryng Robyn hym to,
    And no man do hym dere.

60 John toke his leve at oure kyng,
    The sothe as I yow say;
  The next way to Notyngham
    To take, he yede the way.

61 Whan John came to Notyngham
    The yatis were sparred ychon;
  John callid up the porter,
    He answerid sone anon.

62 "What is the cause," seid Litul Jon,
    "Thou sparris the yates so fast?"

"Because of Robyn Hode," seid [the] porter,
    "In depe prison is cast.

63 "John and Moch and Wyll Scathlok,
    For sothe as I yow say,
  Thei slew oure men upon our wallis,
    And sawten us every day."

64 Litull John spyrred after the schereff,
    And sone he hym fonde;
  He oppyned the kyngus prive seell,
    And gaf hym in his honde.

65 Whan the scheref saw the kyngus seell,
    He did of his hode anon:
  "Wher is the munke that bare the letturs?"
    He seid to Litull John.

66 "He is so fayn of hym," seid Litul John,
    For sothe as I yow say,
  He has made hym abot of Westmynster,
    A lorde of that abbay."

67 The scheref made John gode chere,
    And gaf hym wyne of the best;
  At nyght thei went to her bedde,
    And every man to his rest.

68 When the scheref was on slepe,
    Dronken of wyne and ale,
  Litul John and Moch for sothe
    Toke the way unto the jale.

69 Litul John callid up the jayler,
    And bade hym rise anon;
  He seyd Robyn Hode had brokyn prison,
    And out of hit was gon.

70 The porter rose anon sertan,
    As sone as he herd John calle;
  Litul John was redy with a swerd,
    And bare hym to the walle.

71 "Now wil I be porter," seid Litul John,
    "And take the keyes in honde:"
He toke the way to Robyn Hode,
    And sone he hym unbonde.

72 He gaf hym a gode swerd in his hond,
    His hed [ther]with for to kepe,
And ther as the walle was lowyst
    Anon down can thei lepe.

73 Be that the cok began to crow,
    The day began to spryng;
The scheref fond the jaylier ded,
    The comyn bell made he ryng.

74 He made a crye thoroout al the town,
    Wheder he be yoman or knave,
That cowthe bryng hym Robyn Hode,
    His warison he shuld have.

75 "For I dar never," said the scheref,
    "Cum before oure kyng;
For if I do, I wot certen
    For sothe he wil me heng."

76 The scheref made to seke Notyngham,
    Bothe be strete and stye,
And Robyn was in mery Scherwode,
    As light as lef on lynde.

77 Then bespake gode Litull John,
    To Robyn Hode can he say,
"I have done the a gode turne for an evyll,
    Quyte the whan thou may.

78 "I have done the a gode turne," seid Litull John,
    "For sothe as I yow say;
I have brought the under grene-wode lyne;
    Fare wel, and have gode day."

79 "Nay, be my trouth," seid Robyn Hode,
    "So shall hit never be;

I make the maister," seid Robyn Hode,
    "Off alle my men and me."

80   "Nay, be my trouth," seid Litull John,
      "So shalle hit never be;
    But lat me be a felow," seid Litull John,
      "No noder kepe I be."

81   Thus John gate Robyn Hod out of prison,
      Sertan withoutyn layn;
    Whan his men saw hym hol and sounde,
      For sothe they were full fayne.

82   They filled in wyne, and made hem glad,
      Under the levys smale,
    And gete pastes of venyson,
      That gode was with ale.

83   Than worde came to oure kyng
      How Robyn was gon,
    And how the scheref of Notyngham
      Durst never loke hym upon.

84   Then bespake oure cumly kyng,
      In an angur hye:
    "Litull John hase begyled the schereff,
      In faith so hase he me.

85   "Litull John has begyled us bothe,
      And that full wel I se;
    Or ellis the scheref of Notyngham
      Hye hongut shulde he be.

86   "I made hem yemen of the crowne,
      And gaf hem fee with my hond;
    I gaf hem grith," seid oure kyng,
      "Thorowout all mery Inglond.

87   "I gaf theym grith," then seid oure kyng;
      "I say, so mot I the,
    For sothe soch a yeman as he is on
      In all Inglond ar not thre.

88   "He is trew to his maister," seid our kyng;
        "I sey, be swete Seynt John,
     He lovys better Robyn Hode
        Then he dose us ychon.

89   "Robyn Hode is ever bond to hym,
        Bothe in strete and stalle;
     Speke no more of this mater," seid oure kyng,
        "But John has begyled us alle."

90   Thus endys the talkyng of the munke
        And Robyn Hode i-wysse;
     God, that is ever a crowned kyng,
        Bryng us all to his blisse!

28

Johnie Cock

Child 114 A; Coffin, p. 104

Johnie was at best a poacher and probably very close to an
outlaw, as Child must have felt when he placed this ballad
immediately before the true outlaw poems. Certainly it is
among the best examples of ballad art and illustrates, as
Gerould points out, not only standard ballad characteristics,
but also a striking mixture of the primitive, or at least early,
and the relatively late. The palmer is a conventional purveyor
of news and gossip, but here he appears in the more sinister
role of gratuitous informer. The sudden and brief appearance
of the sister's son (stanza 15) is puzzling. Traditionally, a
sister's son is his uncle's chief support (Hygelac-Beowulf,
Arthur-Gawain, Charlemagne-Roland, Conchobar-Cuchu-
lainn), but here he is no more than an interested and dis-
criminating observer. There is a remote possibility that if we
had the earliest version of the story we should find a family
feud involved and the sister's son one of the foresters or at
least their partisan. The only North American version of
"Johnie Cock" so far found is from Virginia.

1   Johny he has risen up i the morn,
     Calls for water to wash his hands;
  But little knew he that his bloody hounds
     Were bound in iron bands. bands
     Were bound in iron bands

2   Johny's mother has gotten word o that,
     And care-bed she has taen:
   "O Johny, for my benison,
     I beg you'l stay at hame;
  For the wine so red, and the well baken bread,
     My Johny shall want nane.

3   "There are seven forsters at Pickeram Side,
     At Pickeram where they dwell,
  And for a drop of thy heart's bluid
     They wad ride the fords of hell."

4   Johny he's gotten word of that,
     And he's turnd wondrous keen;
  He's put off the red scarlett,
     And he's put on the Lincoln green.

5   With a sheaf of arrows by his side,
     And a bent bow in his hand,
  He's mounted on a prancing steed,
     And he has ridden fast oer the strand.

6   He 's up i Braidhouplee, and down i Bradyslee,
     And under a buss o broom,
  And there he found a good dun deer,
     Feeding in a buss of ling.

7.   Johny shot, and the dun deer lap,
     And she lap wondrous wide,
  Until they came to the wan water,
     And he stemd her of her pride.

8   He 'as taen out the little pen-knife,
     'T was full three quarters long,
  And he has taen out of that dun deer
     The liver bot and the tongue.

9   They eat of the flesh, and they drank of the blood,
      And the blood it was so sweet,
    Which caused Johny and his bloody hounds
      To fall in a deep sleep.

10   By then came an old palmer,
      And an ill death may he die!
    For he's away to Pickram Side,
      As fast as he can drie.

11   "What news, what news?" says the Seven Forsters,
      "What news have ye brought to me?"
    "I have noe news," the palmer said,
      "But what I saw with my eye.

12   "High up i Bradyslee, low down i Bradisslee,
      And under a buss of scroggs,
    O there I spied a well-wight man,
      Sleeping among his dogs.

13   "His coat it was of light Lincolm,
      And his breeches of the same,
    His shoes of the American leather,
      And gold buckles tying them."

14   Up bespake the Seven Forsters,
      Up bespake they ane and a':
    "O that is Johny o Cockley Well,
      And near him we will draw."

15   O the first y stroke that they gae him,
      They struck him off by the knee;
    Then up bespake his sister's son:
      "O the next'll gar him die!"

16   "O some they count ye well-wight men,
      But I do count ye nane;
    For you might well ha wakend me,
      And askd gin I wad be taen.

17   "The wildest wolf in aw this wood
      Wad not ha done so by me;

She'd ha wet her foot ith wan water,
    And sprinkled it oer my brae,
And if that wad not ha wakend me,
    She wad ha gone and let me be.

18   "O bows of yew, if ye be true,
       In London, where ye were bought,
    Fingers five, get up belive,
       Manhuid shall fail me nought."

19   He has killd the Seven Forsters,
       He has killd them all but ane,
    And that wan scarce to Pickeram Side,
       To carry the bode-words hame.

20   "Is there never a boy in a' this wood
       That will tell what I can say;
    That will go to Cockleys Well,
       Tell my mither to fetch me away?"

21   There was a boy into that wood,
       That carried the tidings away,
    And many ae was the well-wight man
       At the fetching o Johny away.

SUPERNATURAL BALLADS

❧

29

The Wife of Usher's Well

Child 79 A; Coffin, pp. 83-4

As Martinmas is November 11, the very fact that the sons'
hats are of unseasonal birch is enough to indicate that they
are revenants even without the explicit statement that this is
not earthly birch. Much of the pathos of the story comes from
the wife's failure to recognize that her sons have not come
home in flesh and blood but only as brief and spectral guests.
In North America, where the ballad has been very popular,
the story follows a pattern distinct from Child A and is characterized by the fact that the sons are little children, usually
sent away to school, and by an often extreme religious color-
ing. Our version was first printed in the *Minstrelsy of the
Scottish Border,* and there are those who have found in it
traces of Sir Walter's helping hand.

1   There lived a wife at Usher's Well,
    And a wealthy wife was she;
  She had three stout and stalwart sons,
    And sent them oer the sea.

2   They hadna been a week from her,
    A week but barely ane,
  Whan word came to the carline wife
    That her three sons were gane.

3   They hadna been a week from her,
    A week but barely three,
  Whan word came to the carlin wife
    That her sons she'd never see.

4 "I wish the wind may never cease,
        Nor fashes in the flood,
    Till my three sons come hame to me,
        In earthly flesh and blood."

5 It fell about the Martinmass,
        When nights are lang and mirk,
    The carlin wife's three sons came hame,
        And their hats were o the birk.

6 It neither grew in syke nor ditch,
        Nor yet in ony sheugh;
    But at the gates o Paradise,
        That birk grew fair eneugh.

*   *   *

7 "Blow up the fire, my maidens,
        Bring water from the well;
    For a' my house shall feast this night,
        Since my three sons are well."

8 And she has made to them a bed,
        She's made it large and wide,
    And she's taen her mantle her about,
        Sat down at the bed-side.

*   *   *

9 Up then crew the red, red cock,
        And up and crew the gray;
    The eldest to the youngest said,
        " 'Tis time we were away."

10 The cock he hadna crawd but once,
        And clappd his wings at a',
    When the youngest to the eldest said,
        "Brother, we must awa.

11 "The cock doth craw, the day doth daw,
        The channerin worm doth chide;
    Gin we be mist out o our place,
        A sair pain we maun bide.

12   "Fare ye weel, my mother dear!
       Fareweel to barn and byre!
    And fare ye weel, the bonny lass
       That kindles my mother's fire!"

30

The Unquiet Grave

Child 78 A; Coffin, pp. 82-3

Unlike "The Wife of Usher's Well," the present ballad, perhaps because of its slender narrative frame, has been seldom found in the United States. One of the most recent American examples to be printed, that in the *Frank C. Brown Collection* (II 94-5) is uncannily like our version, except that in stanza 5 the line "But my breath smells earthy strong" appears as "But the call of death is strong." Here, surely, is a fastidious taste, coupled, one fears, with a good memory of a printed text. This ballad is not the only instance in which the dead express distaste for a mourning so excessive as to disturb their eternal rest.

1   "The wind doth blow today, my love,
      And a few small drops of rain;
   I never had but one true-love,
      In cold grave she was lain.

2   "I'll do as much for my true-love
      As any young man may;
   I'll sit and mourn all at her grave
      For a twelvemonth and a day."

3   The twelvemonth and a day being up,
      The dead began to speak:
   "Oh who sits weeping on my grave,
      And will not let me sleep?"

4   " 'Tis I, my love, sits on your grave,
        And will not let you sleep;
    For I crave one kiss of your clay-cold lips,
        And that is all I seek."

5   "You crave one kiss of my clay-cold lips;
        But my breath smells earthy strong;
    If you have one kiss of my clay-cold lips,
        Your time will not be long.

6   " 'Tis down in yonder garden green,
        Love, where we used to walk,
    The finest flower that ere was seen
        Is withered to a stalk.

7   "The stalk is withered dry, my love,
        So will our hearts decay;
    So make yourself content, my love,
        Till God calls you away."

31

The False Knight upon the Road

Child 3 A; Coffin, pp. 31-2

Whether or not the wee boy of this corrupt and incomplete ballad, or for that matter its singer, knew that he was matching wits with the devil and that failure would carry him off to hell is an interesting but not material question. Despite erosion and lack of conclusion, the line "A' they that hae blue tails" warrants the presence of the ballad in any selection. "The False Knight" has been rarely found in North America.

1   "O whare are ye gaun?"
        Quo the fause knight upon the road:
    "I'm gaun to the scule,"
        Quo the wee boy, and still he stude.

2   "What is that upon your back?" quo *etc.*
    "Atweel it is my bukes," quo *etc.*

3   "What's that ye've got in your arm?"
    "Atweel it is my peit."

4   "Wha's aucht they sheep?"
    "They are mine and my mither's."

5   "How monie o them are mine?"
    "A' they that hae blue tails."

6   "I wiss ye were on yon tree:"
    "And a gude ladder under me."

7   "And the ladder for to break:"
    "And you for to fa down."

8   "I wiss ye were in yon sie:"
    "And a gude bottom under me."

9   "And the bottom for to break:"
    "And ye to be drowned."

32

Lady Isabel and the Elf-Knight

Child 4 A; Coffin, pp. 32-5

Only in the version which we print, and to a lesser degree in B, does the supernatural element survive. In the other versions, and they are many from both sides of the Atlantic, the man is mortal enough, a seducer, murderer, and thief. He persuades the heroine to elope with him and to take with her a portion of her father's possessions. When they come to a body of water he tells her that he is about to drown her, but that she must disrobe in order that her clothes

may be spared. She pleads modesty and he, with a fatal flaw
of decorum, turns his back and she, sometimes strong by
nature and sometimes given strength by need, pushes him
to his death. The lady returns home, wiser if not sadder,
where she has a brisk dialogue with an inquisitive, intelligent,
but bribable parrot. That there are supernatural beings which
will appear and can appear only when wished for by a
mortal is a well-established tradition of which Marie de
France's lay of *Yonec* is an excellent example. These beings,
however, come not to murder but to love, and this elf-knight
is unusual in his compulsion to kill the impulsive daughters
of kings. We observe that though Lady Isabel can cajole
and charm him, it is with his own weapons that he must
be killed. Because his behavior lacked rationality it was
easy and inevitable for the elf-knight to become a mortal
murderer and thief.

1 Fair lady Isabel sits in her bower sewing,
    Aye as the gowans grow gay
There she heard an elf-knight blawing his horn.
    The first morning in May

2 "If I had yon horn that I hear blawing,
And yon elf-knight to sleep in my bosom."

3 This maiden had scarcely these words spoken,
Till in at her window the elf-knight has luppen.

4 "It's a very strange matter, fair maiden," said he,
"I canna blaw my horn but ye call on me.

5 "But will ye go to yon greenwood side?
If ye canna gang, I will cause you to ride."

6 He leapt on a horse, and she on another,
And they rode on to the greenwood together.

7 "Light down, light down, lady Isabel," said he,
"We are come to the place where ye are to die."

8 "Hae mercy, hae mercy, kind sir, on me,
Till ance my dear father and mother I see."

9   "Seven king's-daughters here hae I slain,
     And ye shall be the eight o them."

10 "O sit down a while, lay your head on my knee,
     That we may hae some rest before that I die."

11 She stroak'd him sae fast, the nearer he did creep,
     Wi a sma charm she lulld him fast asleep.

12 Wi his ain sword-belt sae fast as she ban him,
     Wi his ain dag-durk sae sair as she dang him.

13 "If seven king's-daughters here ye hae slain,
     Lye ye here, a husband to them a'."

33

Kemp Owyne

Child 34 A

The wicked stepmother is a stock character in popular literature and she is often addicted to the transformation of her stepchildren, as evidenced, among many cases, by the Queen of Spain in the admirable fourteenth-century English romance, *William of Palerne or William and the Werewolf*. Disenchantment, especially the restoration of youth and beauty by faith and love, is equally common, and here one naturally thinks, though there are obvious differences, of Chaucer's *Wife of Bath's Tale* and its analogues. It is less common for the witch or warlock to be aware of reversal and even, as in "Kemp Owyne," of the probable instrument of defeat. In the ballad the ritualistic nature of the disenchantment, heightened by the use of incremental repetition, is especially prominent. "Kemp Owyne" has not as yet been found in North America.

1   Her mother died when she was young,
        Which gave her cause to make great moan;
    Her father married the warst woman
        That ever lived in Christendom.

2   She served her with foot and hand,
        In every thing that she could dee,
    Till once, in an unlucky time,
        She threw her in ower Craigy's sea.

3   Says, "Lie you there, dove Isabel,
        And all my sorrows lie with thee;
    Till Kemp Owyno come ower the sea,
        And borrow you with kisses three,
    Let all the warld do what they will,
        Oh borrowed shall you never be!

4   Her breath grew strang, her hair grew lang,
        And twisted thrice about the tree,
    And all the people, far and near,
        Thought that a savage beast was she.

5   These news did come to Kemp Owyne,
        Where he lived, far beyond the sea;
    He hasted him to Craigy's sea,
        And on the savage beast lookd he.

6   Her breath was strang, her hair was lang,
        And twisted was about the tree,
    And with a swing she came about:
        "Come to Craigy's sea, and kiss with me.

7   "Here is a royal belt," she cried,
        "That I have found in the green sea;
    And while your body it is on,
        Drawn shall your blood never be;
    But if you touch me, tail or fin,
        I vow my belt your death shall be."

8   He stepped in, gave her a kiss,
        The royal belt he brought him wi;
    Her breath was strang, her hair was lang,

And twisted twice about the tree,
And with a swing she came about:
"Come to Craigy's sea, and kiss with me.

9 "Here is a royal ring," she said,
"That I have found in the green sea;
And while your finger it is on,
Drawn shall your blood never be;
But if you touch me, tail or fin,
I swear my ring your death shall be."

10 He stepped in, gave her a kiss,
The royal ring he brought him wi;
Her breath was strang, her hair was lang,
And twisted ance about the tree,
And with a swing she came about:
"Come to Craigy's sea, and kiss with me.

11 "Here is a royal brand," she said,
"That I have found in the green sea;
And while your body it is on,
Drawn shall your blood never be;
But if you touch me, tail or fin,
I swear my brand your death shall be."

12 He stepped in, gave her a kiss,
The royal brand he brought him wi;
Her breath was sweet, her hair grew short,
And twisted nane about the tree,
And smilingly she came about,
As fair a woman as fair could be.

34

The Daemon Lover

Child 243 F; Coffin, pp. 138-40

The various versions of this ballad, often called "James Harris," from the reassuringly respectable name of the lover, show an interesting process of rationalization. In all probability the "lover" was originally the devil; then, as in our text, a revenant, though here the cloven hoof survives; and finally, as in most American versions, a thoroughly human seducer, usually a sailor and often rich, who lures away the impressionable wife of a carpenter, ship or house. In these later versions the sinking of the ship is a normal hazard of seafaring life and not necessarily even a punishment for adultery. To what extent our version, which first appeared in Scott's *Minstrelsy*, may have been improved it is hard to say. An interesting, if unconsciously burlesqued, example of the vengeful dead lover's return is "Alonzo the Brave and the Fair Imogene" which M. G. Lewis embedded in *The Monk*.

1 "O where have you been, my long, long love,
    This long seven years and mair?"
   "O I'm come to seek my former vows
    Ye granted me before."

2 "O hold your tongue of your former vows,
    For they will breed sad strife;
   O hold your tongue of your former vows,
    For I am become a wife."

3 He turned him right and round about,
    And the tear blinded his ee:
   "I wad never hae trodden on Irish ground,
    If it had not been for thee.

4   "I might hae had a king's daughter,
        Far, far beyond the sea;
    I might have had a king's daughter,
        Had it not been for love o thee."

5   "If ye might have had a king's daughter,
            Yer sel ye had to blame;
    Ye might have taken the king's daughter,
        For ye kend that I was nane.

6   "If I was to leave my husband dear,
        And my two babes also,
    O what have you to take me to,
        If with you I should go?"

7   "I hae seven ships upon the sea—
        The eighth brought me to land—
    With four-and-twenty bold mariners,
        And music on every hand."

8   She has taken up her two little babes,
        Kissd them baith cheek and chin:
    "O fair ye weel, my ain two babes,
        For I'll never see you again."

9   She set her foot upon the ship,
        No mariners could she behold;
    But the sails were o the taffetie,
        And the masts o the beaten gold.

10 She had not sailed a league, a league,
        A league but barely three,
    When dismal grew his countenance,
        And drumlie grew his ee.

11 They had not saild a league, a league,
        A league but barely three,
    Until she espied his cloven foot,
        And she wept right bitterlie.

12 "O hold your tongue of your weeping," says he,
        "Of your weeping now let me be;

　　　I will shew you how the lilies grow
　　　　On the banks of Italy."

13　"O what hills are yon, yon pleasant hills,
　　　　That the sun shines sweetly on?"
　　　"O yon are the hills of heaven," he said,
　　　　"Where you will never win."

14　"O whaten a mountain is yon," she said,
　　　　"All so dreary wi frost and snow?"
　　　"O yon is the mountain of hell," he cried,
　　　　"Where you and I will go."

15　He strack the tap-mast wi his hand,
　　　　The fore-mast wi his knee,
　　　And he brake that gallant ship in twain,
　　　　And sank her in the sea.

35

Thomas Rymer

Child 37 A; Coffin, p. 55

In a poem existing in a fifteenth-century manuscript, Thomas of Erceldoun, usually identified as a thirteenth-century Scot and sometimes credited with the authorship of a Tristram romance, makes a trip to fairyland with its queen and returns with the gift of prophecy. The appeal of the prophecies, if nothing else, gave the poem wide popularity, and from it sprang the present ballad which contains, naturally enough, more popular and traditional elements than does its source. Only one American version has been found, reduced to six stanzas, in North Carolina. Scholars have pointed out evidence to suggest that Chaucer's Sir Thopas, who reverses normal procedure by going uninvited to fairyland to seek out an elf-queen, owes something to Thomas.

1 True Thomas lay oer yond grassy bank,
    And he beheld a ladie gay,
A ladie that was brisk and bold,
    Come riding oer the fernie brae.

2 Her skirt was of the grass-green silk,
    Her mantel of the velvet fine,
At ilka tett of her horse's mane
    Hung fifty silver bells and nine.

3 True Thomas he took off his hat,
    And bowed him low down till his knee:
"All hail, thou mighty Queen of Heaven!
    For your peer on earth I never did see."

4 "O no, O no, True Thomas," she says,
    "That name does not belong to me;
I am but the queen of fair Elfland,
    And I'm come here for to visit thee.

        ❧   ❧   ❧

5 "But ye maun go wi me now, Thomas,
    True Thomas, ye maun go wi me,
For ye maun serve me seven years,
    Thro weel or wae as may chance to be."

6 She turned about her milk-white steed,
    And took True Thomas up behind,
And aye wheneer her bridle rang,
    The steed flew swifter than the wind.

7 For forty days and forty nights
    He wade thro red blude to the knee,
And he saw neither sun nor moon,
    But heard the roaring of the sea.

8 O they rade on, and further on,
    Until they came to a garden green:
"Light down, light down, ye ladie free,
    Some of that fruit let me pull to thee."

9   "O no, O no, True Thomas," she says,
      "That fruit maun not be touched by thee,
  For a' the plagues that are in hell
      Light on the fruit of this countrie.

10   "But I have a loaf here in my lap,
      Likewise a bottle of claret wine,
  And now ere we go farther on,
      We'll rest a while, and ye may dine."

11   When he had eaten and drunk his fill,
      "Lay down your head upon my knee,"
  The lady sayd, "ere we climb yon hill,
      And I will show you fairlies three.

12   "O see not ye yon narrow road,
      So thick beset wi thorns and briers?
  That is the path of righteousness,
      Tho after it but few enquires.

13   "And see not ye that braid braid road,
      That lies across yon lillie leven?
  That is the path of wickedness,
      Tho some call it the road to heaven.

14   "And see not ye that bonny road,
      Which winds about the fernie brae?
  That is the road to fair Elfland,
      Where you and I this night maun gae.

15   "But Thomas, ye maun hold your tongue,
      Whatever you may hear or see,
  For gin ae word you should chance to speak,
      You will neer get back to your ain countrie."

16   He has gotten a coat of the even cloth,
      And a pair of shoes of velvet green,
  And till seven years were past and gone
      True Thomas on earth was never seen.

36

The Three Ravens

Child 26; Coffin, pp. 52-4

There is a striking contrast between this poem and its companion piece, "The Twa Corbies," in which hound, hawk and lady are all unfaithful and the corbies eat the corpse. The poem has not been recorded often in Britain, and in North America we have only "The Three Black Crows," a minstrel stage version which is somewhat like a burlesque of the older form. As evidence of the antiquity of parts of our text one may cite the "earthen lake" of stanza 8, which one recent critic calls "inexplicable," where "lake" means "pit" or "grave" after Latin *lacus* and is not noted by the *New English Dictionary* after 1506.

1   There were three ravens sat on a tree,
       Downe a downe, hay down, hay downe
    There were three ravens sat on a tree,
       With a downe
    There were three ravens sat on a tree,
    They were as blacke as they might be.
       With a downe derrie, derrie, derrie, downe, downe

2   The one of them said to his mate,
    "Where shall we our breakefast take?"

3   "Downe in yonder greene field,
    There lies a knight slain under his shield.

4   "His hounds they lie downe at his feete,
    So well they can their master keepe.

5   "His haukes they flie so eagerly,
    There's no fowle dare him to come nie."

6   Downe there comes a fallow doe,
      As great with yong as she might goe.

7   She lift up his bloudy hed,
      And kist his wounds that were so red.

8   She got him up upon her backe,
      And carried him to earthen lake.

9   She buried him before the prime,
      She was dead herselfe ere even-song time.

10 God send every gentleman,
      Such haukes, such hounds, and such a leman.

37

The Maid and the Palmer

Child 21 A

Since the palmer is God taken on human guise (stanza 11;
a sixteenth-century English proverb asserts that "God is a
good man") and since continental versions have the maid
a blend of the woman of Samaria and Mary Magdalene, perhaps this ballad could be classified as religious. Were it not
for the fact that God, to whom nothing is impossible, is
involved one would conclude that the penances are so difficult that the maid can never be maiden again. A common
English proverb has it that "Old maids lead apes in hell,"
so it is not without paradox that this is one of the things
the maid must do. When one considers the history, characters, and content of the ballad, the nonsensical gaiety of its
refrain is impressive. The ballad is rare in Britain and has
not been found on this side of the Atlantic.

1   The maid shee went to the well to washe,
          Lillumwham, lillumwham!

The mayd shee went to the well to washe,
   Whatt then? what then?
The maid shee went to the well to washe,
Dew fell of her lilly white fleshe.
   Grandam boy, grandam boy, heye!
Leg a derry, leg a merry, mett, mer, whoope, whir!
   Drivance, larumben, grandam boy, heye!

2   While shee washte and while shee ronge,
   While shee hangd o the hazle wand.

3   There came an old palmer by the way,
   Sais, "God speed thee well, thou faire maid!

4   "Hast either cupp or can,
   To give an old palmer drinke therin?"

5   Sayes, "I have neither cupp nor cann,
   To give an old palmer drinke therin."

6   "But an thy lemman came from Roome,
   Cupps and canns thou wold find soone."

7   Shee sware by God & good St John,
   Lemman had shee never none.

8   Saies, "Peace, faire mayd, you are forsworne!
   Nine children you have borne.

9   "Three were buryed under thy bed's head,
   Other three under thy brewing leade.

10   "Other three on yon play greene;
   Count, maid, and there be 9."

11   "But I hope you are the good old man
   That all the world beleeves upon.

12   "Old palmer, I pray thee,
   Pennaunce that thou wilt give to me."

13 "Pennance I can give thee none,
    But 7 yeere to be a stepping-stone.

14 "Other seaven a clapper in a bell,
    Other 7 to lead an ape in hell.

15 "When thou hast thy penance done,
    Then thoust come a mayden home."

HUMOROUS BALLADS

❦

38

Our Goodman

Child 274 A; Coffin, pp. 144-5

Humor is not common in the ballads and some critics would seem to feel that Mr. Child might well have used the presence of much comedy as an excuse to exclude the songs which contain it. Certainly "Our Goodman" (see Introduction, p. v) is deficient in narrative element, but it is an excellent example of cumulative or incremental repetition. Anti-feminism, more common in earlier literature than today, is evident: a woman, caught in misconduct, always has an explanation, and even though her explanation is rejected, she passes on to a new position of effrontery and abuse. Thus would Chaucer's Wife of Bath have dealt with an over-curious husband, except that Dame Alice would have given shorter shrift. The ballad has been popular in America, but usually expurgated by the singer for the collector or by the collector for the press. One collector was informed that there were several "vulgar" stanzas which the singer had omitted since joining the church.

1   Hame came our goodman,
        And hame came he,
    And then he saw a saddle-horse,
        Where nae horse should be.

2   "What's this now, goodwife?
        What's this I see?
    How came this horse here,
        Without the leave o me?"

Recitative. "A horse?" quo she.
  "Ay, a horse," quo he.

3 "Shame fa your cuckold face,
      Ill mat ye see!
    'T is naething but a broad sow,
      My minnie sent to me."

  "A broad sow?" quo he.
  "Ay, a sow," quo shee.

4 "Far hae I ridden,
      And farer hae I gane,
    But a sadle on a sow's back
      I never saw nane."

5 Hame came our goodman,
      And hame came he;
    He spy'd a pair of jack-boots,
      Where nae boots should be.

6 "What's this now, goodwife:
      What's this I see?
    How came these boots here,
      Without the leave o me?"

  "Boots?" quo she.
  "Ay, boots," quo he.

7 "Shame fa your cuckold face,
      And ill mat ye see!
    It's but a pair of water-stoups,
      My minnie sent to me."

  "Water-stoups?" quo he.
  "Ay, water-stoups," quo she.

8 "Far hae I ridden,
      And farer hae I gane,
    But siller spurs on water-stoups
      I saw never nane."

9   Hame came our goodman,
      And hame came he,
  And he saw a sword,
      Whare a sword should na be.

10   "What's this now, goodwife?
      What's this I see?
  How came this sword here,
      Without the leave o me?"

   "A sword?" quo she.
   "Ay, a sword," quo he.

11   "Shame fa your cuckold face,
      Ill mat ye see!
  It's but a porridge-spurtle,
      My minnie sent to me."

   "A spurtle?" quo he.
   "Ay, a spurtle," quo she.

12   "Far hae I ridden,
      And farer hae I gane,
  But siller-handed spurtles
      I saw never nane."

13   Hame came our goodman,
      And hame came he;
  There he spy'd a powderd wig,
      Where nae wig shoud be.

14   "What's this now, goodwife?
      What's this I see?
  How came this wig here,
      Without the leave o me?"

   "A wig?" quo she.
   "Ay, a wig," quo he.

15   "Shame fa your cuckold face,
      And ill mat you see!

'T is naething but a clocken-hen,
   My minnie sent to me."

"Clocken hen?" quo he.
"Ay, clocken hen," quo she.

16 "Far hae I ridden,
     And farer hae I gane,
  But powder on a clocken-hen
     I saw never nane."

17 Hame came our goodman,
     And hame came he,
  And there he saw a muckle coat,
     Where nae coat should be.

18 "What's this now, goodwife?
     What's this I see?
  How came this coat here,
     Without the leave o me?"

"A coat?" quo she.
"Ay, a coat," quo he.

19 "Shame fa your cuckold face,
     Ill mat ye see!
  It's but a pair o blankets,
     My minnie sent to me."

"Blankets?" quo he.
"Ay, blankets," quo she.

20 "Far hae I ridden,
     And farer hae I gane,
  But buttons upon blankets
     I saw never nane."

21 Ben went our goodman,
     And ben went he,
  And there he spy'd a sturdy man,
     Where nae man shoud be.

22   "What's this now, goodwife?
      What's this I see?
  How came this man here,
      Without the leave o me?"

"A man?" quo she.
"Ay, a man," quo he.

23   "Poor blind body,
      And blinder mat ye be!
  It's a new milking maid,
      My mither sent to me."

"A maid?" quo he.
"Ay, a maid," quo she.

24   "Far hae I ridden,
      And farer hae I gane,
  But lang-bearded maidens
      I saw never nane."

39

The Farmer's Curst Wife

Child 278 B; Coffin, pp. 148-50

"The Farmer's Curst Wife" is anti-feministic, though less slanderously so than "Our Goodman." When Chaucer's Merchant, married only two months and off on a pilgrimage, confides to his fellow travellers that if his wife were coupled to the Devil she would overmatch him, he is not attributing to the lady a unique illness of disposition or strength of character. The story of how a woman can be too much for the Devil has been found in various forms from ancient India to present-day America. Although the temptation has been great to consider it a migratory motif originating in

Asia, its nature is such as to justify â belief in the possibility of independent origins. In many instances, perhaps in the primary form of the present ballad, a man has made a pact with the Devil which he can keep only by his wife's readier wit or by her temporary presence in hell. An analogue is the sad story of the fiend Belphegor who, in experimental mood, marries a woman and finds her too much for hell. Mr. Child prints only two versions, of which ours, though imperfect, is by far the livelier. The ballad has been recorded far more often in North America than in Britain, and its popularity here may be due to our Puritan predisposition to see the Devil put in his place. Burns' "Kelly Burn Braes," a reworking of the traditional ballad, may have influenced our version.

1 The auld Deil cam to the man at the pleugh,
     Rumchy ae de aidie
  Saying, "I wish ye gude luck at the making o' yer sheugh.
     Mushy toorin an ant tan aira.

2 "It's neither your oxen nor you that I crave;
  It's that old scolding woman, it's her I must have."

3 "Ye're welcome to her wi' a' my gude heart;
  I wish you and her it's never may part."

4 She jumpet on to the auld Deil's back,
  And he carried her awa like a pedlar's pack.

5 He carried her on till he cam to hell's door,
  He gaed her a kick till she landed in the floor.

6 She saw seven wee deils a' sitting in a raw,
  She took up a mell and she murdered them a'.

7 A wee reekit deil lookit owre the wa':
  "O tak her awa, or she'll ruin us a'."

8 "O what to do wi' her I canna weel tell;
  She's no fit for heaven, and she'll no bide in hell."

* * *

9   She jumpit on to the auld Deil's back,
         And he carried her back like a pedlar's pack.

* * *

10   She was seven year gaun, and seven year comin',
         And she cried for the sowens she left in the pot.

40

Get Up and Bar the Door

Child 275 A; Coffin, pp. 145-6

If the Italian version of this story given by Giovanni
Straparola in his *Facetious Nights* (1555) is any indication,
the present ballad was less innocent in its earlier form. The
plot, however, is such as to permit indelicacy to enter easily
and some versions, including one picked up by Burns and
several from North America, are more suggestive than the
one we give. In any case, humor and human nature are
happily blended, and we feel that Chaucer could have used
the story admirably for one of his *fabliaux*.

1   It fell about the Martinmas time,
         And a gay time it was then,
     When our goodwife got puddings to make,
         And she's boild them in the pan.

2   The wind sae cauld blew south and north,
         And blew into the floor;
     Quoth our goodman to our goodwife,
         "Gae out and bar the door."

3   "My hand is in my hussyfskap,
         Goodman, as ye may see;
     An it shoud nae be barrd this hundred year,
         It's no be barrd for me."

4 They made a paction tween them twa,
 They made it firm and sure,
That the first word whaeer shoud speak,
 Shoud rise and bar the door.

5 Then by there came two gentlemen,
 At twelve o clock at night,
And they could neither see house nor hall,
 Nor coal nor candle-light.

6 "Now whether is this a rich man's house,
 Or whether is it a poor?"
But neer a word wad ane o them speak,
 For barring of the door.

7 And first they ate the white puddings,
 And then they ate the black;
Tho muckle thought the goodwife to hersel,
 Yet neer a word she spake.

8 Then said the one unto the other,
 "Here, man, tak ye my knife;
Do ye tak aff the auld man's beard,
 And I'll kiss the goodwife."

9 "But there's nae water in the house,
 And what shall we do than?"
"What ails ye at the pudding-broo,
 That boils into the pan?"

10 O up then started our goodman,
 An angry man was he:
"Will ye kiss my wife before my een,
 And scad me wi pudding-bree?"

11 Then up and started our goodwife,
 Gied three skips on the floor:
"Goodman, you've spoken the foremost word,
 Get up and bar the door."

BIBLIOGRAPHY

❧

TEXTS

Ballads and Sea Songs from Nova Scotia, collected by W. Roy Mackenzie (Cambridge, Harvard University Press, 1928).

Ballads and Songs Collected by the Missouri Folk-Lore Society, edited by H. M. Belden. University of Missouri Studies, XV, 1, 1940.

Bishop Percy's Folio Manuscript, edited by John W. Hales and Frederick J. Furnivall, 3 vols., with a Supplement of "Loose and Humorous Songs" (London, 1867-68).

British Ballads from Maine: The Development of Popular Songs, with Texts and Airs, by Phillips Barry, Fannie H. Eckstorm, and Mary W. Smyth (New Haven, Yale University Press, 1929).

English and Scottish Popular Ballads, edited by Francis James Child, 5 vols. (Boston, Houghton, 1883-98).

English and Scottish Popular Ballads, edited from the collection of Francis James Child by Helen C. Sargent and George Lyman Kittredge (Boston, Houghton, 1904).

English Folk Songs from the Southern Appalachians, collected by Cecil J. Sharp and edited by Maud Karpeles, 2 vols. (London, Oxford University Press, 1932).

Frank C. Brown Collection of North Carolina Folklore, edited by Newman I. White and others, 5 vols. (Durham, North Carolina, Duke University Press, 1952-   ). [Volumes II and III contain texts of the ballads and songs, whose music will appear in volume IV, not yet issued in 1954.]

Last Leaves of Traditional Ballads and Ballad Airs, collected in Aberdeenshire by the late Gavin Greig and edited . . . by Alexander Keith. Aberdeen University Studies, 100, 1925.

Minstrelsy of the Scottish Border, etc., [by Walter Scott] 3 vols. (Kelso, 1802-03, and many subsequent editions).

Ozark Folksongs, collected and edited by Vance Randolph,

4 vols. (Columbia, State Historical Society of Missouri, 1946-50.)

Reliques of Ancient English Poetry, etc., [by Thomas Percy] 3 vols. (London, 1765, and many subsequent editions).

Traditional Ballads of Virginia, edited by Arthur K. Davis, Jr. (Cambridge, Harvard University Press, 1929).

STUDIES

Coffin, Tristram P., *The British Traditional Ballad in North America.* Publications of the American Folklore Society: Bibliographical Series II (Philadelphia, 1950).

Entwistle, William J., *European Balladry* (Oxford, Clarendon Press, 1939).

Gerould, Gordon H., *The Ballad of Tradition* (Oxford, Clarendon Press, 1932).

Gummere, Francis B., *The Popular Ballad* (Boston, Houghton, 1907).

Hodgart, M. J. C., *The Ballads* (London, Hutchinson's University Library, 1950).

Hustvedt, Sigurd B., *Ballad Books and Ballad Men* (Cambridge, Harvard University Press, 1930).

Pound, Louise, *Poetic Origins and the Ballad* (New York, Macmillan, 1921).

Wells, Evelyn K., *The Ballad Tree* (New York, Ronald Press, 1950).

Wimberly, Lowry C., *Folklore in the English and Scottish Ballads* (Chicago, University of Chicago Press, 1928).

RECORDINGS

A Bibliography of North American Folklore and Folksong, by Charles Haywood (New York: Greenberg, 1951).

A List of American Folksongs Currently Available on Records, compiled by the Archive of American Folksong of the Library of Congress (Washington, Library of Congress, 1953).

Check-list of Recorded Songs in the English Language in the Archive of American Folk Song to July, 1940, 3 parts (Washington, Library of Congress, Music Division, 1942).

GLOSSARY

a' all
a: a wot I know
a of
a to
abon, aboone above
ae one
after the way on the road
airn iron
an on
an', and if
atweel I know well, *i.e.*, of
    course
aucht: wha's aucht? who owns?
ava of all
aw all
awkwarde backhanded, oblique

ba ball
badgers pedlars
bale, balys trouble
ban band, bond
ban bound
barne man
basnet, basnit helmet
belive at once
ben in, within, into the inner
    room
benison blessing
bent grassy field, heath
bete amend, better
billie brother
birk birch
blane stopped
blinkit looked
blinne stop
bode-words message
boote aid, remedy
bore hole

borrow ransom
bot and and also
bouks bodies
bowne make ready
boÿs bows
bra, braw handsome, fine, brave
brae brow
braid plain, clear
brain insane
brand sword
brast burst
braw. *See* bra
breake (one's heart) disclose
    one's thoughts
brether brothers
broad breeding
broken men outlaws
brook enjoy, keep
brotch brooch
bryttlynge cutting up (of the
    deer)
bugelet small bugle
burning shining, glowing
busk prepare, dress
buske, buss bush
but and and also
but if unless
by pay for
byckarte shot (arrows)
byre cowshed
bystode, hard bystode hard
    pressed

ca' call
can (*for* gan) did
capull-hyde horsehide
carlin, carline (old) woman
cast plan

143

chamer chamber
channerin grumbling
chays hunting-ground
chiel child
childer children
cleading clothing
clocken-hen sitting hen
cloth-yard yard (36 inches)
corbie raven
cors curse
cowthe could
crae crow
curch kerchief

dag-durk dagger, dirk
dang struck
dee do
deight, dight, dyght prepared, dressed, brought
Deil devil
den deep hollow, ravine
dere harm
dey die
dight. *See* **deight**
dinna do not
doen, doen her gone
dowie, dowy dismal, dreary, sad
downa do not wish to
dre, dree, drie suffer, endure, hold out, manage (to go)
dress prepare, array, clothe
drie. *See* **dre**
drumlie gloomy
dule sorrow
dune done
dyght. *See* **deight**
dynte stroke, blow

ee, een eye(s)
eir, or eir before
emys uncle's

fa fall
fa: shame fa shame befall
fache fetch
fadge dumpy (woman)
faine: for faine for joy

fairlies wonders
fall: faire might you fall good luck to you
fallow reddish yellow
farley, ferly strange, unusual
fashes troubles
fause false
ferd fear
fere: on fere together
ferly. *See* **farley**
fettle make ready, plan
filinge soiling
fley frighten
forbye nearby
forehammers sledge-hammers
forsters foresters
freyke, freckys man, men
fu full
furs furrow

gab mouth
gae. *See* **gie**
gae, gaed, geid, gane go, went
gaire gore, part of garment
gane. *See* **gae**
gang go, walk
gar, gard, garrd, garde cause, make
garl ?gravel
gate road, path
gaun going
gaw gall
geid. *See* **gie**
genty pretty, genteel
gi, gie, gae, geid, gien, gin give, gave, given
gif if
gin if
girds hoops
glamourie magic
glede live coal, ember
glent moved quickly
gleuves lances, bills, swords
golett throat
good-brother brother-in-law
goud gold
gowans common daisies

graff graft
grat wept
greeting weeping
grevis groves
grew hound greyhound
grith safe conduct
gryte great

ha hall
had, haud keep, hold
hae have
halyde hauled
haud. See had
he high
heal hail
hem them
hende, hinde gentle, courteous
hente picked, taken
her their
herry harry, rob
hight promise
hinde. See hende
hinny honey
holland linen
hom. See hem
hondrith hundred
hooly gently, slowly
hope think
houms low lands by a stream
huggell hug
hussyfskap household duties

ilkae, ilkone each, every
infere together
ir are
I'se I shall
i-wysse certainly, indeed

jaw billow wave
jimp slender, neat
jo lover, sweetheart
jow toll, ring

kemp warrior, champion
kems combs
ken, kend know, knew
kepe I be care I to be

kirkwa church wall
kirtle gown, skirt
kye cows

laigh low
laith loathe
lake pit, grave
lamer amber
lane alone, lone
lap, lope, luppen leaped
lauch laugh
lawing tavern bill
layn concealment
layned leaned
lea leave
lead lead roof
leade cauldron, vat
leaned lay down, rested
lear learning
lemman sweetheart, lover
let prevent
lig lie
lightly make light of
limmer strumpet, rascal
ling heather
list: me list (it) pleases me
lither bad
lodging-maill rent
loe love
long of the your fault
longes lungs
loot let
lope. See lap
low flame
lowe hill
luppen. See lap
lyed gave the lie to
lyff-tenant lieutenant
lynde, lyne linden
lyng. See ling

mae more
magger, in the maggers despite
make, makys mate, lover
March-parti Marches, Borders
marl clayish soil
marrow husband, mate

masteryes feats
mat may
maun must
may maiden
meany, menyie company
meet suitable
meikle, muckle great, much
mell mall
menyie. See **meany**
minnie mother
mold ground, earth
monand moaning
mornyng mourning
mort the note of the horn to announce the deer's death
mote might
muckle. See **meikle**
myllan Milanese steel
mylner miller
myneyeple ?gauntlet

neen none
neisten next
next nearest
nie neigh
noder, no noder no other
norland northland, northern
nourice nurse

ousen oxen
owre, half owre half way
owtlay outlaw

pall rich cloth
parti, uppone a parti apart, aside
pat, pitten put
peit peat, fuel
pine pain
pitten. See **pat**
plat intertwined
ploughs, ploughs of land units which one ox-team could plough in a year
porridge-spurtle porridge-stirrer
pricke target, mark
prime sunrise, 6 A.M.
pu'd pulled, picked

puddings sausages
pudding-bree, -broo broth, water in which sausages are boiled

quiere, quire choir
quo quoth
quyrry dead deer
quyte the make it even

radly quickly
raw row
rawstye rusty
reacheles on careless about
rede advice
rede advise
reekit smoked, smoky
reiver robber
riving tearing
rode cross, crucifix
rood rod (5 1/2 yards)
rowd rolled
row-footed hairy-footed or with shoes of undressed leather
rule disorder, misrule

sar, soar sore
saut salt
sawten assault
say try
say saw
scad scald
scoup leap
scoup: shame scoup the devil go (with him)
scroggs brushwood
sell self
semblyde assembled
shawes woods
shear several
shed by parted, separated, flung apart
shee, sheene, shoon shoe(s)
sheene, sheyne lovely
shete a peny shoot for a penny
sheugh trench, furrow
shoon. See **shee**

shot-window window which opens out on a hinge
shradds twigs
shrift confession
shroggs bushes
sic, sicke such
side hillside
siller silver
skinkled glittered
slade forest glade
slight raze, tear down
slogan battle cry
sloken put out, quenched
slon slay
sma' small, slender
soar. See sar
sowens oatmeal slightly fermented, then boiled and eaten
spait flood
sparred closed
sparris close
spauld shoulder
speed help
speer ask
spendyd grasped
splent plate armor
sprente spurted
spurn fight
spyrred. See speer
stage floor, story
stalle standing-place
starkest strongest
stean stone (seat)
stear stir
sterne stern (men)
steven voice
steven: unsett steven unappointed time
stock the side of a bed away from the wall
stour battle
strayght tight
stye path
suar sure
swapte struck
sweavens dreams

syke gully
syne afterwards, then

taen, tane taken
tear ?there
tent watch
tett lock, tuft
the, thé they
the: so mot I the as I may (hope to) prosper
thear those
ther these
thrae through
thrast pushed, crowded
thresel-cock throstle-cock
threw intermingled
thrild rattled
throly fiercely, violently
tift puff
tint lost
tocke ?took
too-hond sworde sword needing two hands
toom empty
tree wood, wooden pole, bar
trew trust
tristil-tre place (tree) of meeting
trusty tree. See tristil-tre
tul until
twaw two
twin'd parted
twinn, in twinn apart, in two
tyde time

ueiwe yew
unbeen nonexistent
unbigged unbuilt

verament truly

wa wall
wae woe
waft weft
wallowt faded, withered
wame womb
wan dark, gloomy

wane ?wagon
warison reward
wat know
water-stoups water-pails
weal make marks or weals on
weed clothes
weel-far'd handsome
well-wight very strong, brave
whaten, whatten what kind of
while at one time
wight, wighty strong, brave
wilfull lost
winna will not
wiss wish
withy willow
won up get up, arise
won, wone one
wone: ful gode wone very many
wons dwells
wood mad
woodweele ?Golden Oriole
wordlye worldly, mortal

worth: woe worth you may woe
　　come to you
wouche injury
wrocken avenged
wrongeous improper, unfitting
wyld wild animals, game
wyte blame

y, one
yae one
yare ready
yate, yett gate
yede went
ye-feth in faith
yerle earl
yerly early
ye'se ye shall
yestreen yesterday evening
yett. See yate
youd went
y'th' in the